One Woman's
Olympic Journey

One Woman's Olympic Journey

Joan Rosazza
Melbourne 1956

First Edition

Designed by Zach Harris
Birds and Kings Creative Enterprises
www.birdsandkings.com

ISBN 978-0-578-87718-1

Eastwood Road Press

eastwoodroadpress@gmail.com

To Ed, backstroker

About Joan Rosazza

Joan grew up in Torrington, Connecticut and started her swimming at the local YMCA. Joan is retired from her teaching career. She and her wife have raised two children, and they live on Cape Cod in Massachusetts.

About the Author

Bill Ryan grew up in Torrington, Connecticut, swam on the YMCA age group team, and the High school swim team (THS '68). Bill is retired and lives in Massachusetts. He swims as a member of US Masters Swimming.

Table of Contents:

Acknowledgments

The author would like to sincerely thank those who helped make this book possible:

Joan Rosazza, whose accomplishments unfold in this book—for the interviews, for the dozens of emails, for access to her "Olympic Journey" letters, and for allowing me to photograph her swimming memorabilia and include them in the book.

I am truly grateful to these friends and family who contributed a great deal to the making of this book: Zach Harris, Paul Bentley, Bishop Peter Rosazza, Jack Rosazza, Sue Mignerey Kearney, Eileen Murphy Mooney, Marc Wilcox, Jon Murphy, John Anderson, Betsy Stengel, Lynn Cabana, Priscilla Ryan, and Elspeth Harris.

Reading Tips

Interviews are shown in italics:

Joan: *Joan Rosazza*

Peter: *Bishop Peter Rosazza—Joan's brother*

Jack: *Jack Rosazza—Joan's brother*

Sue: *Susan Mignerey Kearney—Torrington YMCA swim team member with Joan*

BR: *Bill Ryan (author)*

Letters: Joan wrote 19 letters home to her family in Torrington, Connecticut from Australia. These sections have "Letters" in the title. The letters have been lightly edited for clarity including editorial clarifications in brackets.

Introduction

Two Races for Glory

There are two races knit together in this book. Joan was in both of them.

First, there was the 100-meter freestyle, and five days later the 4 x 100-meter freestyle relay with three of her American teammates. The first race set the stage for a showdown in the second.

In the first race, three Australians, two Americans, a Canadian, a New Zealander, and a South African are vying for the three medals. If they win one, it will be written about in the first paragraph of their obituaries.

The marquee swimming event at the Olympic Games in this era was the 100-meter freestyle. Someone who won this race was unofficially crowned the world's fastest swimmer.

After the first race, anticipation built for a rematch of sorts in the relay. Could a country put together a quartet of sprinters to win a medal? Did they have the depth of talent to make it onto the podium, even if they didn't win a medal in the 100 freestyle?

Joan swam the 100-meter freestyle final on December

1st . To get there she had to swim that race twice over a period of two days, once in qualifying in the field of 35 swimmers, then once again in the semi-finals in a field of 16, only eight of whom would move onto the finals.

To keep that razor sharp edge over three days was arduous. How did each naiad maintain their mental focus for the 60-second-long race, hoping their fine-tuned nerve endings weren't burnt out by anxiety and exhaustion? And as we shall see, unbeknownst to her coach, Joan needed rest.

Joan's letter home about the final of the 100 freestyle described the ninety minutes spent in the locker room ahead of the race and how the tension was broken for some, while not for others. They finished their warm up at 7:00 pm and didn't swim the final until 8:30pm, an eternity in waiting.

Two Australians were the pre-Olympic-Games favorites, Lorraine Crapp, the current world record holder, and Dawn Fraser. They were one or two levels above the other 35 swimmers and everyone knew it. Lorraine Crapp had broken the world record in the 100 freestyle twice, both times eight weeks before, in October, 1956. Dawn Fraser would go on to win Gold in the 100 freestyle in Rome (1960) and Tokyo (1964). This was her debut Olympic Games.

Lorraine Crapp and Dawn Fraser, though they were heavy favorites in the 100 freestyle, were not a guarantee to carry Australia's four-person relay to a win.

Two days passed between the final of the 100 freestyle and the qualifying heat for the 4 x 100 relay. Time for rest.

The relay was the second and final event for Joan Rosazza at these Olympic Games, and the most exciting.

Relay events were controlled bedlam in contrast to the staid, single events. The single events had one swimmer on each of the eight starting blocks, three timers, and the five judges who decided the order of the finish. In the relay, there were 32 swimmers crammed onto the deck area, 24 timers with their stop watches and the five judges. That's 61 people! As each swimmer was coming into the finish of their leg, the judges leaned over to make sure that the next swimmer didn't jump too early. As if this were not chaotic enough, the swimmer that just finished had to quickly exit the pool, where they then lingered in the mass of their teammates cheering and yelling, sidestepping the timers and judges, until the last swimmer touched the wall.

It is no wonder that this relay was considered to be the best and most exciting race of all the events, for both the men and the women.

Chapter 1

The Beginning

"How did a girl raised in a town with no sports for girls get to stand on the medal box at the Olympic Games and receive a Silver Medal from the Prince of Denmark? Not on her own."

- Joan Rosazza

Joan Rosazza has given her inspirational, 'Not on Her Own' speech many times over the years.

Born in 1937 in Torrington, Connecticut, Joan grew up with three brothers and played sports with them and their neighbors in the backyard, in the street, and wherever else they could. Except Joan could not play organized sports, like her brothers did, because there weren't any for girls. There were literally no opportunities for girls in organized sports in the 1950s in Torrington, Connecticut. There were no Little League baseball teams, no swim teams, no basketball teams, no track, and no high school sports for girls.

Joan was fortunate, playing baseball with her brothers. But when her brothers played Little League, Joan could only watch from the stands.

That all ended one day when Doris Murphy, an ex-Olympian swimmer who lived in Torrington, arrived at the YMCA pool and started the first girls swim team.

Joan: *My mother was very big on exercise. During the winter, we four siblings couldn't get outside and exercise that much, so she sent us all to the YMCA to swim. I hated it, because I was so cold all the time. What I did was, I would get into my bathing suit, put my hand in the water, sit out, and take a shower afterward. When I went home she'd say, "Did you go in?" Now my Irish mother had told us kids, "If you lie to your mother, when you die your hand will stick out of the grave." I knew I couldn't lie, so I would say, "I was in the water."*

Then one day this woman appeared. She told all of us girls that we had to line up and swim one lap, so I was nailed. It was Doris Murphy of course. I got in there and swam for my life, and she told me I was on the swim team.

Three Doors that Opened for Me

BR: *So, did you know Doris Murphy before she walked into the pool that day?*

Joan: *No, I think they had come to town fairly recently. I know she swam at night at the Y, and my mother did too. She told me about this fabulous swimmer who was in the Olympic Games.*

But I didn't quite make the connection when she appeared; and God bless her because I talk about three doors that opened to me. The first was my family because my family didn't have any problem with me doing sports of which there were none for girls. The second was Doris Murphy, my first coach. The third was Dick Papenguth, the swimming coach at Purdue.

Growing up we would play all kinds of sports in the backyard.

After supper in the summer, my brothers and I would play kick-ball with all the neighbors. We couldn't wait to get out and play. We made up rules: a ground-rule-double in the catalpa tree... keep the ball out of mister what's-his-name's yard because he'd come out and yell at us, and we'd make someone else go get it.

But there were no sports for girls. I could throw a baseball; my big brother would make me go out and throw a baseball with him if there was no one else around. We'd play baseball at home. I saw two of my brothers get into Little League and I'd have to sit in the stands.

BR: *I went to an age-group YMCA swim meet recently to watch a friend's daughter swim. She's six years old. I checked the heat sheets and 70% of the swimmers were girls and 30% were boys.*

Joan: *Isn't that something?*

Sue Mignerey Kearney, a Y swim team member with Joan, weighs in on age group swimming in the '50's

BR: *How was your Y swim team experience under Doris Murphy?*

Sue: *We were originally "Open Swim" swimmers. Then, Doris became our teacher. I fortunately was able to do well in my swimming. I was young, 12 or 13 years old. At 13 I won a junior national championship in the 100 freestyle at a meet at Yale University[*].*

Maybe you remember the old Payne Whitney Gymnasium and pool at Yale? It was beautiful. I remember going down to have Bob Kiphuth[**] look at my stroke. I still have good visual memories of that pool. I loved the pool, deep all the way.

BR: *I swam in the Yale pool as an age-group kid and I always swam*

---

[*]   New Haven, Connecticut

[**]   Yale men's swim coach

poorly because it was so deep, I was just scared of it. And, the spectator area was huge.

Sue: *Yes, with all the seating going way up. There were caverns everywhere. It's interesting you didn't like the pool. I loved it. It was deep all the way. That makes it faster.*

We went to New York City for meets. That was a long way to go from Torrington. There weren't that many girls swim teams back then. I was a freshman in high school.

I could find my way to the old Torrington Y pool; if it is still there?

BR: *It is still there, but it is empty of water and used for storage. They built a new 25-yard pool in 1968.*

Sue: *(laughs) Oh, interesting.*

Torrington YMCA Girls Swim Team Members, December 1949
Front Row L-R: Eileen Murphy, Claire Cummings, Sally Lamphier, Alice Fitch,
Donna Beecher, Content Ellis, Janet Mignerey, Joan Rosazza, and Beatrice Minetto
Back Row L-R: Judy Toussaint, Fay Dressel, Maureen Murphy, Susan Mignerey,
Mary Lou Schneider, Shirley Minor, Ann Caravati, and Cathy Ashe

I knew I had a Chance for the Olympic Games

*1954 Florida Amateur Athletic Union (AAU) Nationals
Junior year in high school.*

Doris Murphy, Joan Rosazza, Bea Minetto, and Sandra Ruwet from Torrington traveled by train to "AAU Swimming Nationals" in Daytona Beach. It was a 24-hour train ride. The girls slept in their seats. Joan was entered in the 100-yard freestyle where she came in 10th place with a time of 1:02.

*1955 Florida AAU Nationals
Senior year in high school.*

Doris and Joan and some other Torrington girls travel again to Florida for the AAU Nationals.

Joan was again competing in the 100-yard freestyle. This time she came in 3rd with a time of 0.59, breaking the all-important 60 second barrier, which only eight women in America across all age groups had done at the time.

Joan: *One great thing about Doris (Murphy) is she had a wide vision of swimming. She would take us to AAU meets in New York and New Jersey. When I was a Junior in high school, she took four of us down by train to Florida to Nationals. I think I had a breakthrough, and I was swimming about a minute two (1:02.0) in the 100-yard freestyle. I came in 10th place. We came back next year and all of a sudden, I did a "59 something."*

BR: *Wow.*

Joan: *I know! And I was third. So, I knew I had a chance for the Olympics.*

BR: *Did you meet swimmers from Purdue at Nationals?*

Joan: *Yes, I met some of them and thought it would be a good place to swim and get an education. There wasn't this college pressure that there is nowadays.*

I remember John Hogan*, calling me into his office and saying, "This is the only school you applied to?" and I said, "Yes." He said, "Well, you got in."

BR: *Did Doris ever say to you, "You have Olympic potential?"*

Joan: *No. She never talked about that. Neither did Pappy.***

BR: *In 1984, the Los Angeles Olympic Committee interviewed former Olympians living in the LA area, and Doris Murphy was one of them. In the interview Doris said she started the girls swim team in Torrington, and they became the best in Connecticut, but you were the only potential National level swimmer, so, I was thinking she may have discussed that with you. She brought you to Florida twice.*

Joan: *And the second time when I broke 60 seconds, I was third too. I think there were only eight women in the US at that time, maybe fewer, who had broken a minute.*

BR: *So, did you push yourself?*

Joan: *Oh yeah.*

BR: *Did you have competition in Torrington?*

Joan: *It was different. I didn't love practice. Swimming practice can be the most boring thing in the world. I mean, you can't chat with people. You're in the water...*

BR: *...Obviously, you can't hear well.*

Joan: *Yeah, exactly...*

BR: *...And, in a race, you can't see all eight lanes.*

---

*   Torrington Superintendent of Schools

**   Dick (Pappy) Papenguth, Women's Swimming Coach, Lafayette Swim Club, and Men's Swimming Coach at Purdue University

Joan: *No, you can't see at all.*

I decided this... I really wanted to make the Olympic team. And in order to do that—I didn't know if I could but—the one thing I never wanted to happen was to say that I never tried my hardest in practice. And so that was my philosophy. And it didn't matter who I was racing in practice, or what my time was when I was racing. I had to give my all, all the way. If I didn't make the Olympic team I knew I did the best I could. Once I made the team, even if I didn't medal, I carried that philosophy with me.

Chapter 2

Joan's First Coach

Doris O'Mara Murphy was a member of the USA Women's Olympic Swim Team at the 1924 Summer Games in Paris, France. She was 15 years old. Doris was selected for the 100-meter backstroke and in the 4 x 100-meter freestyle relay.

The USA Olympic Team traveled to Europe by ship—the "SS America." There were no Trans-Atlantic air flights; Charles Lindbergh wouldn't complete his solo flight to Paris until 1927. The US Olympic Committee built a custom, make-shift, canvas-sided swimming pool on the upper deck of the ship. It was tiny; only two swimmers could practice at any one time and they had to tie a rope around each of their waists so they would swim in place. That was the extent of swim practice on the ocean voyage to Paris. Meanwhile, the US Track athletes could run around the ship on the Promenade Deck.

*Swimmers with golf clubs! Doris O'Mara (Murphy) 3rd from the right,
Gertrude Ederle 3rd from the left The rest of the swimmers are unidentified*

*Aboard the S.S. America enroute to the 1924 Paris Olympic Games
Front Row L-R: Eleanor Holm, Doris O'Mara (Murphy), Gerturde Ederle.
Back Row L-R: Johnny Weissmuller, Buster Crabbe, (possibly) Duke Kahanamoku*

Chapter 3

The Vast Void

In the 1940s and '50s there was a vast void in organized women sports in America. But there were cracks in the void...

In the summer of 1920, Doris O'Mara, a 12-year-old from Yonkers, NY, was summering with her family in an ocean beach house in Milford, Connecticut. At her older brothers' urging, she entered an open water swim meet organized by the local lifeguards. She was given a head start in her race because she was younger than the other competitors. She came in 2nd. The meet announcer noticed her promising performance and recommended Doris to the Women's Swimming Association in New York City, which, with time and training, gained Doris an Olympic berth on the USA women's team at the Paris Olympic Games in 1924.

In the late 1940s, Doris O'Mara Murphy, now married with children and living in Torrington, Connecticut, walked onto the deck of the YMCA's 20-yard pool and started a girl's swim team. Joan Rosazza was there putting her hand in the water to pseudo-participate in "Open Swim."

~~~~~~

Lafayette, Indiana, late 1940s: Dick Papenguth, the Purdue University Men's Swimming Coach, started a women's swim team. They practiced at the Purdue swimming pool, but otherwise, the team received no support or recognition from the school. He named the team "Lafayette Swim Club," a women's college swim team without the college.

~~~~~~

In 1953, Stan Tinkham, a 22-year-old Army Private stationed in Washington, D.C., was chosen to be the coach of a women's swim team at the Walter Reed Army Medical Center's indoor pool. The daughters of military personnel stationed there brought the team into existence the previous year. The first coach left in a dispute after one year, leaving the vacancy that Stan filled.

Over the next three years three women on Tinkham's team developed into world class swimmers. Shelley Mann, Mary Jane Sears, and Betty Brey made the USA Olympic Team in 1956. They became teammates of Joan Rosazza at the Melbourne Olympic Games, and Stan Tinkham became the Women's Olympic Team Swimming Coach.

~~~~~~

Gender equality in swimming will finally arrive at the Tokyo Olympic Games in 2021, if held. For the first time in 124 years, across 28 Olympic Games, the program of events for women will equal that of men. Since the first modern Olympics in 1896 there has been a 1500-meter freestyle (or equivalent) event for men. In Tokyo 2021 there will, for the first time, be a women's 1500-meter freestyle event.

Chapter 4

How to Swim Freestyle Fast

Here, Joan Rosazza and Sue Mignerey comment on learning swimming techniques back in the Torrington Y days.

BR: *Swimming is all technique. Strength itself is useless without skill. Overcoming drag and resistance is a big part of swimming. Where did you learn your swimming technique?*

Joan: *We had none of that. You just got in and swam. There was no science. It just wasn't happening. What the coach did was organize the workout. I noticed in your notes that you talked about splits.* There were no splits in practice.*

I am a very visual learner. We had Sue Mignerey (Kearney) on the swim team, and everybody used to say, "What a beautiful stroke." I'd watch her like a hawk. I could learn from watching. My body could learn by watching. That helped me a lot.

Sue: *(laughs) I didn't really know that. I'm still swimming now at age 86. Wherever I swim people always say, "You have a beautiful stroke". Maybe it's true, I don't know.*

---

*　　　Interim time checks during swim workouts.

13

I swim a mile a day seven days a week. Now we're in lockdown.* I was working out with a team in New York. I'm a swimmer. That's my therapy... back and forth, back and forth, back and forth. At my age now I don't do it as intensely as I used to... but, I swim.

Over the years different coaches have told people, "Watch Susan's stroke"... I don't even know what I'm doing. I'm just swimming. Maybe we can attribute Joan's stroke to me, but I don't know. (laughs)

BR: *I'm really glad to hear that people are still saying, "Watch Sue swim, she has the perfect stroke."*

Sue: *(laughs) Peter (Rosazza) still swims. We still talk on the phone about swimming.*

BR: *Joan wrote letters home from Melbourne to Torrington. Those letters had to cross the Pacific, and they arrived much later than the event, so the family, and everyone else had to find out the results from the newspaper.*

Sue: *I have memories of that. Now there is instant communication, which to me is a miracle.*

BR: *She used airmail and she wrote on that really flimsy air mail paper.*

Sue: *Oh, that paper, oh my gosh.*

BR: *Joan, any technique coaching at Purdue?*

Joan: *Yes, at Purdue, Pappy (Papenguth) would often tell me relax. This was not often, because he didn't talk that much. He'd say, "Relax your shoulders, relax."*

He also had us swimming with open hands.

The theory was, not that much water passes through the fingers, and open hands give you a wider pull. And he also had us not rush through in the water. If you're doing it right it would be like an

―――――――――

*   Due to COVID-19 pandemic. Interview conducted in February 2021.

"S."

Pappy's theory was, by catching the water, not just traveling through it, your speed increases.

Resting, Tapers, and Adrenaline

In competitive swimming, two swimming distances are used: 100-yards and 100-meters. Most swimming pools in the United States are 25-yards long. Most pools in all other countries are either 25-meters or 50-meters long. One meter is about 10% longer than one yard, so the elapsed time for a 100-meter freestyle race will be greater than a 100-yard freestyle race by about 10%. The swimming events at the Olympic Games are held at a 50-meter pool. In this Chapter, when Joan says, "a 59 something" she means the 100-yard freestyle. Joan broke one minute in the 100-yard freestyle in 1955. Only seven other Americans had broken the 60 second barrier at that time. In 1956 no woman in the world had broken 60 seconds for the 100-meter freestyle until Dawn Fraser swam a 59.9 100-meter freestyle in October 1962.

BR: *The pre-meet rest period—the taper—you needed that.*

Joan: *Yes, Pappy (Papenguth), had this figured out. When he took us down to Nationals in Florida in 1956, I got the flu. I couldn't swim for three days before my event. I did a 59 something (for 100-yards).*

He figured out that I needed a long rest before I competed. In other words, some people could go in and just drive themselves right up to the day of the meet. I couldn't do that.

BR: *So, you needed a longer taper.*

Joan: *Yeah, or just out of the water.*

BR: *That's what they call a "drop-dead taper". Just don't swim for* *seven days.*

Joan: *(laughs) I didn't know the name for that. Really?*

BR: *Yes, tapers are individualized these days and you needed that long rest.*

Joan: *Yeah, and Pappy got that.*

There was no real communication between Stan Tinkham and Dick Papenguth. So, Stan didn't realize my need for more rest.

BR: *They didn't talk?*

Joan: *No, no. Of course, there was no email. (laughter)*

I was pretty tired by the time I swam. Looking back, you can figure things out. I never had it in my head to say I needed to rest. I would never say that to a coach either.

BR: *It's more scientific now. They take blood samples and analyze everything that's in there.*

Joan: *I wonder if it's too much, I don't know. They don't do that (blood sampling) in high school.*

BR: *I see swimmers come back to masters competition in their 30's and 40's, who were burned out in college, swimming 40,000-yards a week. But they got over that and came back to swim again.*

Joan: *You won't have any shoulders left.*

Chapter 5

The Earthquake in Women's Sports

At the 1956 Olympic Games 99 women competed in swimming compared to 136 men, which isn't a poor showing considering that female athletes made up only 13% of the participants across all sporting disciplines in Melbourne. The share of female participants has risen steadily since then to reach 45% across all sports in 2016.

What happened in the intervening 58 years? What enabled or encouraged more women and girls to participate in swimming and other sports?

Part of the answer is the US Federal Law, "The Higher Education Act of 1972" and the special section called "Title IX." It has proven to be a landmark piece of legislation.

To sum up Title IX: "No person in the United States shall, on the basis of gender, be excluded from participation in, be denied the benefits of, or be subjected to discrimination under any education program or activity receiving federal financial assistance."

Title IX covers all educational activities, but it has had a singular effect on women's collegiate sport. Basically, if a college or university has a men's athletic team, it must also have a women's team. If men receive athletic scholarships, women must also. Women's Field Hockey is often the offset for Men's Football. Title IX became a turning point in opportunities for women in collegiate athletics, which was pretty near zero before 1972.

Joan: *Did you want to talk about Title IX?*

BR: *Oh yeah, that would be good.*

Joan: *It definitely changed sports completely for females. Definitely. There were no sports in college of a high level, or elementary school, but I was also a coach at that time (1972). I coached in Winchester, Massachusetts and the state also had Massachusetts General Law 603, which had similar protections as Title IX.*

The women coaches of girls were not getting the same salary as the coaches of boys, nor were we getting the same amount of time, nor did we have a locker room, and the trainer was at the boys' locker room, and all that was part of the history, and that's understandable.

I talked to the coaches of girls' sports and told them I was going to file a class action suit against Winchester. I was pissed off. They really didn't want much part of it. I said here's what you can do; you can pay me to park in Boston. It cost them $5. I went to the Massachusetts Commission against Discrimination and filed the case. It took a while; it wasn't one of their hot issues. I kept bugging them and they finally signed an agreement. We didn't go for back wages, just saying from now on, if you coach girls in this town, you get the same if you are coaching boys. That changed so much because then it changed the amount of time for the sports. It opened up new sports for girls. I was coaching softball, gymnastics, and field hockey. I was a busy woman. As I think back, I don't know how I did it. (laughs)

We won and that was good. It was good for us, and it was good for the kids too. Some of the men coaches didn't like it. They said you're going to take money away from boy's sports.

I was told, "You're not going to find enough people to do the sports," and, "Girls don't like sports."

My first teaching job was in Evanston, Illinois. It was a fabulous school, 4,000 students. Best school I ever taught in. It was really outstanding. But in the whole state of Illinois girls couldn't do sports. It was a law to protect the health of girls because competition is so hard for them, and so unhealthy. There were ten women in our Phys-Ed department. I was an Olympian, and there was a former Olympic gymnast on the staff too.

"Protect us from ourselves," or something like that.

I had very strong feelings about it. Definitely.

Once passed into law, Title IX faced fierce opposition in college sports, especially within the NCAA (National Collegiate Athletic Association). Walter Byers, Executive Director of the NCAA is quoted as saying, "We'll throw $1 million into the war chest to defeat this piece of legislation."

Christine Grant, athletic director at Iowa State University, was a particular stand-out in advocating for passage of, and then overcoming the residence to, Title IX.

In an interview about Christine Grant, Vivian Stringer, hall of fame basketball coach at Rutgers said, "She's a giant among giants."

And, Charles West, former athletic director Southern Illinois, said, "If you were to ask me who has done the most in this country, in terms of opportunities for women in sport, I'd say, Christine Grant, Christine Grant, Christine Grant—those would be my first three answers."

Chapter 6

Motoring in the Motor City

August 7th through 10th
Brennan Pool, Detroit, Michigan

Brennan Pool was an outdoor venue. One archive photo shows the Trials at night, under the lights.

Fifty-seven top American female freestyle sprinters came to Detroit to vie for one of the three spots on the Olympic Team in the 100-meter freestyle.

For the 100-meter freestyle event at the Olympics, getting to the medal stand was a three-step dance.

1. Qualifying heats where all swimmers competed
2. Semi-finals where the top 16 swimmers competed
3. Final where the top eight swimmers competed

But, at the Olympic trials in Detroit in 1956, the semi-final step was skipped. This created tremendous pressure on all fifty-seven swimmers in the qualifying heats. Only the top eight would advance to the final, instead of the top 16 to a semi-final. While it is uncommon for a swimmer seeded low in qualifying to make the final, it has been done in the past.[*]

Shelly Mann's time in the qualifying heats, 1:04.6, was one-tenth off the world record. It was a new American Record, breaking the one that had stood since 1945.

	Shelley Mann	**Joan Rosazza**	**Nancy Simons**
Qualifying Heat	1:04.6	1:05.3	1:05.6
Place	1st	2nd	3rd
Final	1:05.6	1:05.2	1:05.1
Place	3rd	2nd	1st

Joan also swam in the 400-meter freestyle at the Olympic Trials, "on a lark." Shelly Mann and Joan were the only two swimmers to make the finals in both the 100 and the 400 at the Trials, a testament to their skill and fitness.

BR: *Was your family able to go to Detroit for the trials?*

Joan: *My parents weren't going originally because my grandfather was suffering from cancer. He passed away. After the funeral mom and dad got in the car and drove out. I didn't expect that and it was great.*

Doris and Jack Murphy came to the trials along with their son, Johnny Murphy. My parents were surprised to see Johnny. They

---

* At the 2008 US Olympic Trials, Morgan Scroggy was seeded 41st in the 200 backstroke. Incredibly, she made the final as one of the top eight swimmers. No one before her had accomplished that feat. Morgan was no flash in the pan. She competed in three Olympic trials, 2004, 2008, and 2012. At the 2021 trials, for Tokyo, to limit the size of the entrants due to COVID-19, the meet was broken into two meets, Wave One and Wave Two. The second wave was for the top-level elite swimmers, who had the best chance to make the Olympic team. USA Swimming set the cutoff between Wave One and Wave Two at the 41st fastest swimmer, this being a nod to Morgan's amazing accomplishment in 2008. It could be named the "Morgan Scroggy Line."

got the biggest kick out of him, because he was just so relaxed about life and everything. The Rosazzas and the Murphys ended up staying in the same motel and did a little socializing. My father, who was usually tightly wound, could not believe how relaxed Doris and Jack were about everything. My Dad kept mentioning it.

In Detroit the qualifying swims were one day and the finals the next day. The qualifying was pressure packed because, with no semi-final, only the top eight swimmers would advance to the final. And only the top three in the final would swim the 100 in the Olympics.

BR: *You had to swim in 50-meter pools. Was that a big adjustment?*

Joan: *Yeah, it was hard. After I made the team in August we weren't leaving (for Australia) until November. I knew Bob Kiphuth from Yale, (the men's swim coach). He was pretty gruff. He took a liking to me, and there was an upstairs 50-yard pool at Yale. He'd let me come down and practice on my own. I wasn't very good at practicing on my own. I'd get in there and try. But it's not the same as being coached.*

BR: *When you finished the Trials you didn't travel to Colorado, all expenses paid, training camp, nutritionists, and physical therapists?*

Joan: *(laughs) No. It didn't exist. There was a team Shelley Mann was on; there were five or six of them from that team, not many. Their coach was Stan Tinkham, who became the USA Women's Olympic swimming coach. He had me come down and swim at the Walter Reed pool, which was a 50-yard pool. I practiced for three weeks before going out to Los Angeles.*

BR: *Have you visited the Indianapolis University—Purdue University pool? It was build in 1982. It's name was abbreviated to IUPUI, and was pronounced "Ooo-eee-poo-eee." It's now just the IU pool.*

Joan: *No, I haven't. (laughs)*

BR: *I was there in 1986. At one end of the pool is a mezzanine-level, glass-enclosed room that displays the IU and PU Swimming Wall of Fame. That's where I saw a photo of you taking a racing stance in the old Torrington Y pool. Remember the Lion's Head at the shallow end of the pool?*

Joan: *(laughs) Oh yes. Oh my god. There are probably not many pools like that.*

BR: *I instantly recognized the Lion's Head before I read the description and then I recognized you. I didn't know you went to Purdue. It was a surreal moment.*

Joan: *My one regret was this... I never won a Varsity Letter. I never could win a letter. I've been meaning to write them but haven't gotten around to it.*

BR: *You could say, "My picture is in the Wall of Fame."*

Joan: *Well, they know. I think they know all that. I don't know if they realize what it was like then. We were all part of Purdue.*

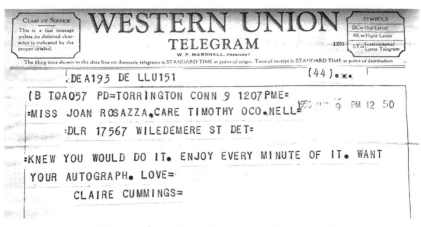

Congratulatory telegram from Claire Cummings, a Torrington Y swimming team-mate of Joan's on her making the USA Olympic Team

Dick "Pappy" Papenguth Biography

From the International Swimming Hall of Fame:

"The late Dick Papenguth 'Pappy of Purdue,' was eminently successful as a swimming coach, a diving coach, an actor-producer of water shows, and as an administrator at camp, club, college, national and Olympic levels. He is credited with being the first swimming coach who 'worked college women hard.' It paid off with world records and national championships won by his Lafayette Swim Club, which was made up of Purdue co-eds. He was the first in a line of great coaches at the Indianapolis Athletic Club. His coaching career began in 1925 and ended with his death in 1970 at age 67.

1921-1925	*University of Michigan diver and swimmer*
1926-1939	*Coach at Indianapolis Athletic*
1939-1970	*Coach at Purdue University and Lafayette Swim Club*
1952	*Olympic Games women's swimming and diving coach, Helsinki, Finland*

Coached four Olympians, nine world record holders, eight Diving Champions, more than 60 All Americans and at least 40 US National Champions"

Chapter 7

Apollo and Jupiter

The end-to-end trip from Connecticut to Australia took 42 hours flying including refueling stops, plus overnight stopovers. In 1956, many nations sent their teams by ocean liner to Australia.

When Joan and her teammates left Los Angeles destined for Melbourne they would cross the International Date Line and the Equator. Back in the day, Pan American World Airways printed up fancy Roman and Greek god themed certificates for each passenger in commemoration. When Joan crossed the Date Line she, and all passengers and crew, lost a day, which coincidently was her parents wedding anniversary, November 12th.

Letter: Leaving LA

Friday November 9, 1956

Hi All,

We're finally on our way. As you can tell by the

stationary, I'm trying to save money on stamps. They're pretty expensive.

Last night everyone was running around like crazy trying to get packed, send luggage home and get to bed early. There was an awful heat wave in LA and it was hard to sleep. The temperature reached 95 yesterday. This morning we got up at 6:00 and weighed our luggage. Mine came to only 29 lbs. which means I have room for souvenirs. Then we ate and got into buses which took us to the airport. There were a whole lot of people there for the sendoff. Everyone was taking movies and pictures. I took a lot myself. Then we got on the plane and here I am, over the Pacific.

We're all eager to see Hawaii. Stan [Tinkham] said he has five workouts planned. I'm going to talk to him because everyone feels that our stay here is so short, we should get to see things and do things. Our first workout is supposed to be tonight.

I took movies out the window of the plane. If they come out, they'll be really neat. I'll try and mail them home from Hawaii. There are 12 of us in the front compartment of the plane. My seat mate is my teammate, Sylvia Ruuska. As soon as the plane took off, we changed into Bermudas so we're a bit more comfortable. They just finished serving us sort of a brunch and we ate like pigs.

Oh! The Kappas* from USC came down to see Marley [Shriver] and me off. They gave us Gardenia corsages and wrapped up a package for each of us. Marley got water wings and I got an inner tube. I thought that was so nice of them.

---

*   Kappa Kappa Gamma (KKG), Women's College Sorority

I'll close now. Happy Anniversary again Mom and Dad. Sorry I can't be with you. In fact, we never get to see November 12 because that's when we cross the International Date Line.
Love,
Me

Crossing the International Dateline certificate from Pan American World Airways: "Domain of Phoebus Apollo: Know all peoples that Joan Rosazza, once earthbound and time laden, is now declared a subject of the realm of the sun and of the heavens, with the freedom of our sacred eagle..."

USA Women's Swimming and Diving Teams, leaving Los Angeles, November 1956.

Letter: Leaving Hawaii

Sunday November 11, 1956

HAPPY ANNIVERSARY

Dear All,

We've just taken off from Hawaii and everyone hated to leave. I've never in my life had such a fabulous time.

When we arrived, there were several hula dancers to greet us and they gave us orchid leis. There are so many flowers in Hawaii and the whole place just smells so beautiful. After receiving the leis and welcomes, we got onto a bus and were driven to the Royal Hawaiian Hotel with a military motorcycle escort.

Let me tell you a bit about the islands. There are seven islands and Oahu is the biggest. It's pronounced "ow-aa-hoo". We flew over the other islands and landed at Oahu. Hawaii is the next largest island, but it has only 1/10th the population of Oahu. The capital city on Oahu is Honolulu and that's where Waikiki beach is. Our hotel was right on the beach. The island is very hilly and mountainous and there are trees all over—palm trees, banana trees, pine trees, etc. The native tree is the monkey rubber which is beautiful. They make all sorts of salad bowls, etc. out of them. The mountains used to be volcanoes and you can see the hardened lava.

All in all, we had only 50 hours in Hawaii, but we sure made use of the time. As soon as we arrived at the hotel, we got our suits on and went in the ocean. (By the way, the hotel room rate is $36 per night for a couple.) The Pacific is fabulous. The waves are big and the water is warm. I had to wear my tank suit in the water. We rode waves and it was a ball. The thing you have to be careful of is the coral. It's hard and sharp and some of it is poisonous.

You'll have to get used to this crazy writing paper.* After our dip (the plane got in at 4:30 pm), we ate dinner. This was at 6:45. The dining hall is beautiful. It overlooks the sea and they have these huge glass sliding doors which open toward the sea. Some are open and you get the clean breeze and can hear the waves. It really gives you an appetite. We had special Olympic menus. Of course, I have one for a souvenir.

---

*   Overseas air paper

There was just meat on the menu, but they gave me fish—delicious. It's called Mahi-Mahi, some south sea fish. We have our own bottled water. I'm going to steal a bottle. I have so many souvenirs, we'll have to add another room to the house. Stan [Tinkham] had said we were to be ready to workout at 7:30, so with full stomachs, we went to workout. We were scared to death it would be hard, but Stan said all we should do is loosen up so we felt good. Neat, eh?

We got back from the pool at 9:30. Stan had told us that we were working out at 9:00 am and 4:30 pm. Were we ever thrilled. When it was 9:30 pm in Hawaii, it's 11:30 pm in LA, so we were pretty tired. I went to sleep at 10:00 pm and slept through until 8:00 the next morning.

In our room we had a veranda and two screen doors which opened onto it. I slept with the window open and the air was so beautiful. What a difference compared to the stinky downtown LA air. (Hope you're not bored with the details.)

We ate breakfast at about 8:30, and immediately after Nancy Simons and I went shopping. Let me tell you, it was quite a shopping tour. I bought a lot and had fun doing it—none of the usual guilty feelings. By the way, you should all be getting some mysterious looking packages from Hawaii in about three or four weeks. I bought myself some things, namely a Hawaiian shirt, dories, a neat bathing suit and a uke. I sent the uke home.

Here's the deal. Nancy Simon's grandfather was an admiral in the Navy and he is a very close friend of Governor King who is the governor of Hawaii and has been for over 16 years.* His wife Pauline phoned Nancy and wanted to take her around the island and then to lunch. She said Nancy could bring a friend and so I went. At 11:15 a huge chauffeur driven Packard drives up to the Royal Hawaiian. It was Pauline King and her daughter. We drove over quite a bit of the island. We saw the upside-down falls where the water flows up. Then we stopped at Pali which is on a mountain 1100 feet above sea level. It's really windy up there.

After our sightseeing (oh, we went to Pearl Harbor too) we went to the governor's mansion and it is a mansion. It was the former home of Queen Liliuokalani who was the last and probably the most famous ruler of Hawaii. They've kept a lot of the atmosphere. They have a lot of her furniture which is in great condition. They also have some silver which was given Queen Lilli by Napoleon III. I was quite impressed.

Then the governor walked in and we met him. He's quite a man—personal friend of Ike's you know. All five of us had luncheon at the Oahu Country Club. I felt quite important, parading around with the governor. After lunch it was about 2:00 and they took us back to the hotel. Oh! They gave us each an orchid lei—purple orchids.

Meanwhile, back at the Royal Hawaiian, we got into our new bathing suits and ran to the beach. The USOC** got us surf boards for free. Bully of them! We rode the waves for an hour and a half. If you catch a wave right, it will carry you 100 yards. I tried standing up on the

---

*   Hawaii and Alaska were not states in 1956. They were territories until statehood was established in 1959.

**   United States Olympic Committee

board but was unsuccessful. It was still loads of fun.

Then we ran from the beach, grabbed our tank suits and tore to practice. The workout was fairly hard, especially since everyone had spent several hours in the ocean. After practice, we ate dinner in the lush dining room. They had a Hawaiian band and Hula dancers for entertainment. After dinner, several of us walked to Don, The Beachcomber's. It's a very famous restaurant, not far from the Royal. It's no building, but it looks like a tropical jungle and it has all sorts of thatched and straw huts where people eat—loads of atmosphere.

We ran back to the hotel, put on our new Hawaiian clothes and walked the beach until 10:00 pm.

Most of the hotel dining rooms overlook the beach, so we were able to peek in windows and catch the floor shows. You should have seen the one girl do the Hula. What a wiggle!

I awoke at 6:30 and at 6:50 went to Mass with Lana Miki, a Hawaiian girl who swims. The church was kind of outdoors. There were no walls, just a straw roof. I thought it was inspiring to attend Mass there.

Our workouts for the day were scheduled for 8-10 am, and 1-3 pm. When we got back to the hotel after Mass it was ten to eight and everyone was ready. They screamed at us to rush because Stan said that if everyone was on time, we'd workout only once. Fortunately, everyone was on time.

ALOHA!

The workout wasn't too bad. As soon as we got back to the hotel, we ate breakfast. At 11:00 Maureen Murphy and I went body surfing for an hour. Then we ate lunch and went back in the water. We had a ride in an outrigger canoe. That's even more fun than surfing.

There are about seven in the canoe plus the steersman who is a Hawaiian. We'd get the canoe way out and then when we'd see a wave coming, everyone paddles like mad. Then the wave catches the canoe and you stop paddling and ride the wave. You go really fast and over 200-yards. In fact, you can ride the wave all the way to shore. Then when you're paddling back out, you're going against the waves. So, the canoe front goes way up in the air and then crashes down. I got in the front seat and really got a ride.

After the outrigger, went for the surf boards again. Once a series of waves came at us and they were enormous. All I could do was hang on to the surf board. It's something to see the waves come at you, especially when they're about 10' when they break. That seems mighty big. You have to watch out for flying surf boards. I love to live dangerously.

Then, unfortunately, it was 3:30 and we had to pack to leave. Boy, did I hate to leave. You'll have to come here someday, Mom and Dad. What a paradise.

We had to go thru customs and show our passports to get on the plane. After we took off, the stewardess showed us how to work the life savers—in case we ended up in the Pacific. It's now 9:25 pm Hawaiian time and we expect to refuel at Nadi, one of the Fiji Islands, at 3:30 am. It should be quite hot as Nadi is right near the equator. We missed November 12 when we crossed the International Date Line.

Have a happy anniversary even though I'll never see the day.

I'll close now and write again later. (Writer's cramp, you know.)

Love,

Joan

    p.s. I've learned to play bridge.

Crossing the Equator certificate, Pan American World Airways:
"...Know all ye by these presents that, Joan Rosazza, on this 11th day of November in the
year of 1956 was borne on the wings of a clipper of the Pan American World Airways
across the equator..."

Letter: Arriving in Melbourne

Thursday November 15, 1956

Dear All,

    I'm finally here and let me tell you I've had experiences. Just before we landed, the weather got kind of rough but it wasn't too bad. When we landed, we had to throw away all our Hawaiian leis because they were afraid we'd bring bugs into the country. They checked our vaccination and passport and then we got on a bus headed for the village.

In Australia, they drive on the left and the steering wheel is on the right. Several times I thought we were going to crash. Now I'm getting pretty well used to it. Also in Australia, a drug store is called a Chemist, and they don't say something is expensive—it's "dear." The people talk cockney and sometimes you can't understand them.

Every place we go there are thousands of kids who want autographs. The village is something. It's enclosed by an iron fence and there is only one gate which is guarded. This keeps everyone out but the Olympic people. All the women live in one section and there's another fence around the women's quarters. This keeps the men out. No men are allowed inside. I'm in an apartment with Sylvia Ruuska [freestyler] as my roommate. Also in the apartment are [divers] June "Juno" Irwin, Barbara Gilders, Jeanne Stunyo, and Paula Jean Meyers. Downstairs are [swimmers] Mary Anne Marchino, and Maureen Murphy, Carin Cone, and Mary Jane Sears, Shelley Mann, and [Manager] Vee Toner. Next to us are Nancy Simons, and Marley Shriver, Kay Knapp, and Nancy Ramey, [Susan] Dougie Gray, Betty Bray, and [diver] Pat McCormick.

We have no heat or hot water or telephone or TV (TV just came out here last week and downtown everyone stands in front of the store windows and watches it), or radios. All the little boys wear bermudas and knee sox. They have rosy cheeks and all look like they need a haircut.

The French and Italians have wine for dinner and lunch. Nancy Simons and I are trying to work up a deal so we can eat in their dining hall. I've met a lot of Pakistanis and they have the neatest hats made of lamb's wool. I'm trying to work a deal. Yesterday on the bus on the way to the pool, I was talking to this man from Pakistan. He gave me some money, which I'm keeping for Jack, and his card. He's a major. He was telling me all about the Muslim religion, the marriage ceremony etc. of his people. We talked for over a half hour and it was so interesting.

You'll have to pardon this jumbled mess. I'm telling these things as they come into my mind.

I've met several Italians and talked with them in Italian. I'm doing very well. They're kind of forward though. One of them took one of my swap pins and didn't give me anything for it. The Russian girls live in the house in back of ours. I haven't talked to any of them, but they seem very nice. I have talked to the Russian boys.

We've gotten more things since we've been here. Yesterday we got our sweat suits—they are beautiful!—and four tank suits (all fitted), two bathing caps, rubber pool slippers, goggles, wool sox, nose clip, ear plug, and an Olympic towel. We still have to get our parade uniform, a $100 Handmacher* suit, and wool bathrobe.

Hope I can remember what I wrote in the first letter. I sealed it.

The Olympic pool is beautiful and supposed to be very fast. There are eight lanes. Believe it or not, 3,000 people paid two shillings apiece to see us practice

---

*   Handmacher suits were very popular from the 1940s to the 1960s, along with their magazine advertising trademark "Tailored by Handmacher."

yesterday. These people are really swim fans.

A photographer took some pictures of me yesterday. He was from the UPI[*] I think. He said *The Torrington Register* asked for some pictures of me. He took one of me sitting on a starting block, one of me with Maureen Murphy, one of me with a Japanese girl. If you get any, save a lot of copies—o.k.?

We met three British girls: Margaret, Judy, and Barbara. They say, "Oh! That's smashing." How's that for an expression?

When I got here there were three letters and a cablegram for me. The cable was from the pledges of KKG. It said "Dear Roz—The shot of the gun, the cheer of the crowd, Here's success to you, from your sisters so proud."

You should see the food we get. It's better than any I've ever had, except of course yours, Mom. For lunch yesterday we had chicken, for supper we had filets. It's like cafeteria style and we can have as much as we want. I had three filets.

I haven't felt too good swimming, but Stan [Tinkham] said my 50-meter sprints were very good. As soon as I recover from the trip, things should be o.k. Both last night and the night before I had 10 hours of sleep. It's great sleeping weather. The beds are neat.

The Opening Ceremony is a week from today.

So, far I've gotten money from Australia and Pakistan and I should get a lot more, Jack.

Every night they have entertainment for us at the Rec Hall and everyone congregates and socializes. It's loads of fun.

~~~~~~~~~~~

[*] United Press International

I must depart now. Cheerio!

Love,

Joan

p.s. Tom and Jack should be getting mysterious post-cards from Fiji. Pete will get one too.

Oops! This morning at 9:30 we raised the American flag near our quarters. Everyone wore travel uniforms. -Me

Joan Rosazza signing autographs

Letter: The Olympic Village Experience

Saturday November 17, 1956

Dear All,

I'll just have time to start this as we have to practice in a couple of minutes. Jack, I have money from 19 different countries for you including Russia and Hungary. I've been working all sorts of deals to get money and trade swap pins. So, far, I have 19 swap pins—it's almost a record because it's hard to get a lot of pins. In the last letter I said that the Italians were fast and one of them stole a swap pin. Well, last night they had a dance at the Rec Center and the Italian gave me a swap pin and a post card from Rome. They have great music and I danced with him. Let me tell you—he was the best dancer I've ever danced with. He could Charleston, Jitterbug, Bob, Waltz, Tango—everything. I had a great time. He doesn't speak English, but my Italian is very good. I'm working on a deal to eat in the Italian dining room.

Sunday night I have a dinner date with Mr. Chida from Pakistan. I guess I'll have to practice up on my belching. You know it's polite to belch after meals. I still hope to get one of those lamb hats. That would be a real souvenir.

There aren't many amusements around here, but it's wonderful to be able to talk to so many different people. Two nights ago, we met a Hungarian girl named Suzie Ordogh. She spoke only a little English. We invited her to our quarters and afterward we went to the Hungarian quarters. One of the girls there spoke good English and acted as interpreter. We talked for over an hour and was it ever interesting. They talk all about the revolution and how each was affected. They all had revolutionary insignias instead of the ones the Russians gave them. Therefore, they expected some sort of punishment when they returned. And most of them intended to go back. One had just received news that her mother was missing. Another was married and she had a child at home. This one was a 29-year-old swimmer. Another was engaged and wanted to go back to her fiancée. Boy those people have guts. They didn't have any clothes except sweat suits and one change, but when the Australians found this out, they gave them a whole bunch of clothes. I sure wish we could help them in their revolution.

Last night I took a Finnish Sauna bath. They're free around here and they're the greatest. You go in and take off all your clothes. Then the attendant leads you into a room that is hotter than Hades. In the room are wooden racks where you can sit if you want. Also, they have pans of cool water so you can douse yourself if you want. They give you switches of bay leaves to hit yourself with. I'll never know why. Dougie, Nancy and I were together and we all had a ball. There were two Russians in there—one a fencer, the other a chaperone. The chaperone was enormous and had rolls of fat all over herself. You can stay in as long as you want. We could only stand it for about five minutes. Then, we dried off and ran home and jumped into bed. I slept from 9:30 pm to 8:00 am and soundly at that.

Beth Whittall [Canadian freestyler and Purdue classmate] got in yesterday and it was really good to see her. She looked so white compared to us. I guess that between LA and Hawaii I got a bit of a tan. I haven't had a chance to have a good talk with her yet because she was so tired. Unfortunately, she doesn't eat in our dining hall. In a way that's good because there wouldn't be any food for the Americans.

Nestles has a stand right near our house where they serve free coffee and Milo. Milo is a chocolate drink that is delicious. It's especially good because it's hot and of course free.

Vee Toner*, is so funny. We have meetings about every other night and they last for an hour, even though they're about nothing. The other night she appointed a girl from each apartment as "towel chairman." Barb Gilders was appointed from our unit. It was really funny, Jeanne Stunyo stood up and said, "I don't think it's fair. We should elect a towel chairman." We nearly died laughing and Vee, who has no conception of time, was all set to run off an election.

Here's some exciting news. You've no doubt heard of Nina Ponomaryova, the Russian discus thrower who was caught shoplifting some hats in England. Well, yesterday, Nancy, Dougie, and I were walking around the village when a photographer came up to us and asked if we'd mind having our pictures taken with Nina. We said, "Of course not." So, we walked to the track where Nina was practicing. We were introduced and shook hands with her. Then they took two pictures: one was of me pinning an American swap pin on her while Dougie and Nancy watched, and the other was a picture of her showing me how to throw the discus. The later was in the morning's paper. This afternoon, Nancy and I met the photographer again and they gave us copies—which I have. Maybe you saw the picture. They said they sent it to the US—They're with the AP** and UPI.

Anyway, later on, we saw Nina and she beckoned to us to come with her. She took us to the Russian house, no less. There was a comrade chaperone who didn't want us to come in, but Nina said (in Russian—doesn't

---

* USA Women's swim team Manager

** The Associated Press

speak English) we could come and Nina is a big girl. She took us to her room and gave us each a Russian pin. Then she shook hands with us and we left. So, now I have a Russian buddy.

Must close now. Cheerio.

Love,

Joan

Chapter 8

Lighting the Flame

Letter: Opening Ceremony

Friday November 23, 1956

Dear All,

There hasn't been too much excitement so I haven't had much to write about. We did have time trials two days ago and everyone did great except me. I did a lousy 1:08.6 [for the 100-meter freestyle], and nearly died doing it. Hope I come thru in the meet. Nancy did a 1:05.4. Carin did a 1:14.7, only .3 off her American record [for the 100-meter backstroke], and Sylvia did 4:59.1, a full 10 seconds under her American record [for the 400-meter freestyle]. She has a great chance for a gold medal. We'd love to see her beat Lorraine Crapp.

On Monday we had only one workout so Betty Brey and I went shopping. The wool here isn't very cheap at all. In fact, it's almost as expensive as in the States and the styles are funny.

We've been tapering off and doing mostly starts, turns, and sprints. I'm in great condition and should do well, although I haven't in practice.

NOW FOR THE NEWS

Yesterday was the Opening Ceremony. Everyone got all dressed up in her and his parade uniforms. The Americans looked sharp. Then we got into buses. There were 168 buses to take the athletes from the village to the stadium. The stadium is about eight miles away and there were people lined up cheering on the street all the way. We had a huge motorcycle escort. All the way over, we were waving to people.

Then we got into the cricket field which is just outside of the main Stadium. On the field was a sign and a flag from each country. We lined up behind our flag and formed ranks. This was just a practice—as the parade wasn't scheduled to start for two hours. Then we broke ranks and socialized. Down under the Stadium they had a bar, no less. It was hotter than crazy.

So, Nancy Simons and I went down and let this man buy us a beer. Of course, we were taking a chance but it was worth it and I'm sure we weren't the only ones who visited the bar.

Cameras weren't allowed in the Stadium. However, never wanting to say die, I stuffed my little movie camera in the bottom of my purse, put toilet paper over it and then put lipstick, comb, purse, etc. on top of the toilet paper. The purse was a bit heavy, but it worked. I took pictures—25 feet worth—while we waited.

Then we were told to form ranks, as the parade was about to begin. Everyone was bustling with excitement. The order of the parade was Greece first, then everyone alphabetically—with Australia bringing up the rear.

Uruguay was in front of us and USSR in the back.

We Americans—the girls—looked sharp with our red shoes and purses. We marched six abreast and kept in beautiful step. Our left arm swung free and the right thumb was hooked onto the handbag. We marched up to the entrance to the Stadium and then we could hear the band—the royal band of some sort. I had never been in the Stadium before so it was even more impressive. When we marched in the sky nearly came down. 130,000 people screamed and yelled and it brought tears to everyone's eyes. It also made everyone real proud and I was told they liked it the way we marched. On the green in the center were lined up all the teams which preceded us.

As we passed the Duke [of Edinburgh, husband of Queen Elizabeth II], our parade sergeant yelled, "Ready, eyes right," and we looked to the right. The boys looked neat. They had two men standing, one before you came to the Duke and one after. As each line passed the first man, they took off their hats. And as they passed the second, they snapped them back on. NOTE: only athletes were allowed in the parade—no officials or coaches.

We marched around the stadium and into place. Then Russia came. They got quite a cheer.

Next there were a couple of speeches. Everyone's feet hurt so we took off our shoes. Then the Duke opened the Games officially. A report came in that the runner was almost at the stadium. Everyone watched the entrance and he came running in. I tried to get a picture but I was in the back and couldn't do too well. He circled the stadium and then climbed the steps to the torch. He stood for a minute and then lit the torch.

Everyone screamed.

Then they let the pigeons loose. That was about it. We formed ranks and marched out, and took the Olympic oath.

While we were waiting for the runner, we were socializing with the Russians. I have two Russian boyfriends and they came up to me and gave me a Russian pin and a handkerchief which was part of their uniform. I know how to say hello in about 10 languages now.

The India team looked sharp as did the Pakistan team with their turbans.

Boy, do I have souvenirs. When I get home, it should take a week to show you them.

We had a Thanksgiving dinner at 7:00—all the turkey we could eat. It was great. Mary Anne, Maureen, and I went to Mass in the morning at 7:00. It was some Mass. There were 13 people counting the server and the Priest. Officially there is no church service allowed in the village. However, every morning a Priest comes over and says Mass in a room no bigger than our den. We were very close to the altar—no more than three feet away. The Mass took only 25 minutes.

I have a lot to do and so many postcards to send. I've decided not to send many. I think the ones I sent from LA should suffice. There's so much going on and I hate to miss anything.

Got a cablegram from the faculty and students at THS [Torrington High School]. It was very, very nice.

Cheerio for now.

Love, Joan

p.s. Thanks to Tom and Dad for the letters. Hope you're feeling better Dad.

USA Olympic Team uniform scarf

Chapter 9

60 Seconds to Glory

Joan's Melbourne Event Timeline

100-meter freestyle

Nov 29	Nov 30	Dec 1
Qualifying	Semi-finals	**Final**

4 x 100-meter freestyle relay

Dec 2	Dec 3	Dec 4	Dec 5	Dec 6
Practice for the relay	*Practice for the relay*	Qualifying	Rest day	**Final**

Letter: "I swim in two days"

Tuesday November 27, 1956

Dear All,
    Can't remember when I wrote last, but I'll do the

best I can as far as news goes.

First of all—the swimming news. I swim in two days so you'll probably have news of how I did before you get this. If you remember, I said that the rules have been changed and they say that anyone on the swimming, diving, or water polo team is eligible for the relay. Last night we had a swim off at the Olympic pool. As I have told you, my time trials have been terrible—nothing below 1:08. However, I did fairly well in the swim-off. We drew for heats. There were seven trying out—Nancy, Shelley, Marley, Kay, Betty, Sylvia, and me. Stan wanted two heats and we drew for them. I was in the first with Nancy and Sylvia. It was very close and I just touched them out. I was first, Sylvia second and Nancy, third. Our times were 1:05.3, 1:05.4, and 1:05.6 respectively. In the next heat, Shelley was barely first with a 1:06.2. Thus, we four are on the relay. I was beginning to wonder if something wasn't wrong with me and maybe I had lost a bit of my old steam, but I guess not. I know I can go under 1:05 and even if I don't win, I'm pretty sure I can come home with a new American record. The other night Lorraine Crapp swam two hundredths under 1:04. The Australians had a swim off for 4th place on their relay—the first three are definite—Lorraine, Dawn, and Faith Leech. The girl that won did 1:05.8—that's their SLOW woman? I just hope I can anchor our team.

My big race is in two days and I'm not nervous—just excited. It's something to see the way some of the favorites have been upset. I've been to the track [venue] quite a bit. Each time I've sat near Reverend Bob Richards and he's very nice. He won the pole vault yesterday. Tom Courtney won the 800-meters yesterday. He's a Fordham grad. Bobby Morrow won the 200-meters today and the 100-meter dash three days ago—two gold medals!

The boys picked their [4 x 200-meter freestyle] relay last night too. They had a swim off on Saturday. The first three definitely made the team and they were to have another swim off for the 4th place. Ford Konno won easily and did 2:07.0 which is .2 off the American record. He really wanted to make that relay. He joined Bill Woolsey, Dick Hanley, and George Been to round out the 4-man team.

Did I tell you that when we were in Hawaii we met Ford Konno's wife, the former Evelyn Kawamoto who swam on the 1952 Olympic team? By the way, did you get some strange objects from Hawaii? You should have by now.

Thanks for all the letters Dad. Glad to hear you're doing well even though you're bothered by F.F. [fanny fatigue]. I got a nice letter from Pete. That makes two since I've been here. He said you sent him my letters. Please don't lose them. I'm sure I'll enjoy reading them to my grandchildren.

The neatest rumor has been going around that we're going on a world tour in June—our whole team. There's a big meet in Moscow, Russia after which they'd like to take us all over Europe, etc. I sure hope it's true.

Unfortunately, I'm running out of movie film and it costs $5 a roll here. Maybe I'll get one roll, but no more. I have taken about five already. Hope they come out nicely.

Yesterday we met Lew Hoad. He's the Australian tennis player who won at Wimbledon. He's really nice.

Tonight we went over to visit the Hungarians. Eva [Szekely] is the 29-year-old swimmer who speaks good

English. We gave them a whole box of clothes, tank suits, etc. that we all collected. I do believe they were glad to get them. Eva is married and her husband [Dezso Gyarmati], is on the water polo team. She's very beautiful. She showed us pictures of her 2-year-old daughter who is really sweet. Her husband can't go back to Hungary because of the conditions there, so he is going to the US. She's going to try to get her daughter our of Hungary and meet him there. Boy, do they hate the Russians and I mean hate.

Guess what! I found a good buy on men's sweaters and bought Christmas presents for the men of the house. However, I'm so anxious to see everyone and I know I'll be so excited when I get home that everyone might get his Christmas present early. I have no idea of men's sizes and I hope everyone in our family wears a 42, because if they don't, it's just too bad.

One of the girls on the USA track team came in second in the broad jump. Her name is Willye White. She wasn't even expected to make the finals. Everyone's really happy for her.[*]

Did I tell you about my telegrams? I got them from my pledge class, the faculty and students of THS.

Cheerio for now,

Love,

Joan

Swim Practice in Melbourne

The Russian swim team won no medals at the Helsinki

---

[*]　　　Willye White—16 years old at the Melbourne Games, went on to take part in five Olympic Games, two as an athlete.

Olympic Games in 1952. They were in the midst of another terrible showing at these Games. In the end, the men won two bronze medals, the women zero.

All the swimming nations practiced at the newly built Olympic pool, but since there were 235 swimmers from 33 countries, it was difficult to get pool time. All the teams were limited to one-hour sessions, but some Russian coaches and officials spent a lot more time there.

BR: *Were the Russians a force in swimming in Melbourne?*

Joan: *Swimming was one of their poorest sports. They paid very close attention to us in practice. Every time we worked out in the pool a group of Russian coaches and officials would be on hand, taking notes and movies.*

Someone, it could have been me because I think that way, wanted to mess up their film. I asked Stan (Tinkham) if we could do it and he said we could. So, when they were filming, we did two silly things. We swam with our hands made into fists for a while, and then we swam using just one arm for a bit, then just the other arm for a bit. We threw a little fun into those workouts.

Collecting Olympic Pins

Joan: *At the Opening Ceremony our team was next to the Russian team. After the parade of countries, while waiting for the Olympic flame to arrive, we were trading parts of our uniforms. That's when I traded pins with more than one Russian.*

Joan's Olympic pin collection consists of 24 pins, and four of them are from Russia.[*]

[*]   This is a clue to solving the Olympic Pin Photo Quiz in Appendix A.

Letter: 100 freestyle
Swimming the Qualifying Heats

Friday November 30, 1956

Dear All,

Last night was my first swim of the Games and as you probably know, I was second in my heat to Lorraine. She did 1:03.4 and I did 1:05.5. I was a bit disappointed with my time, however, I feel that I'll do much better tonight. I didn't feel a cable was worth sending, but I'll send one after tonight or Saturday.

Tonight are the semi-finals which consist of two heats. In my heat are Dawn Fraser [1:02.4], Faith Leach [1:04.9], Natalie Myburgh [1:05.1], and Helen Stewart [1:07.1]. I can't remember the others, but I believe those are the important ones. Shelley and Nancy are in the second heat.

In the Qualifications, I was 7th. Dawn Fraser [1:02.4], Lorraine Crapp [1:03.4], Faith Leach [1:04.9] [all Australians], Ginny Grant [1:05.1 Canada], Natalie Myburgh [1:05.1 South Africa], Shelley Mann [1:05.4], and me. Nancy Simons did a 1:06.5. I don't think she clutched; she just did a slow time. I was surprised at Shelley's time because she hasn't done too well in practice. However, having once done a 1:04.6 [at the USA Olympic Trials in Detroit in August 1956], I believe she should have done better.

My goal is of course a gold medal and my secondary goal is to beat all the Americans, because I sure would love to go on that World Tour. I felt I was pushing hard yesterday, but there's something harder I can push for— that's the way I feel.

There's not news of much else. Thanks for your cablegram, if I already didn't thank you.

Not much else to say, so Cheerio.

Love,

Joan

Letter: Swimming the Semi-Finals
100-meter freestyle

Saturday December 1, 1956

Dear Family,

Last night were the semi-finals, and now I'm looking forward to the finals tonight. I was 7th in 1:05.9. However, I'm sure you already know this. Nancy Simons didn't make the finals with a 1:06.1. Shelley Mann tied for 5th in 1:05.5 with Ginny Grant of Canada. In 4th place is a girl from New Zealand, Marrion Row, 1:05.3, and the three Australian wonders.

I was a bit disappointed with my time. I was third in my heat to Dawn Fraser and Faith Leech. It's funny, but the meet seems anticlimactic compared to everything else that's been going on—our clothes, the trip, Hawaii, etc. I'm not the only one who feels that way, because a lot of the other girls have said the same thing. The Opening Ceremony was so fabulous that after it, nothing seems to be able to match it. The track is over today. The swimming has swept the track news right off the front pages of the papers. These Australians are really fans.

Last night the Duke of Edinburgh paid an unexpected visit to the pool. I sat right near him. He really enjoyed the meet, especially when the Australian men won the first three places in the 100 free. USA was 4, 5, 6, with Patterson, Hanley, and Woolsey finishing in that order.

Yesterday was the first day of Summer and today the weather is beautiful. Everyone is outside taking sun baths. I nearly dropped when I saw the German and Bulgarian girls sun bathing with only underpants on. They were well inside the village, but it still didn't look just right.

Last night after the meet I had a fish dinner at the International Dining Room. There is only one Italian girl swimmer and she's only 14 years old. She is all alone and she couldn't speak English and was having quite a time with the waitress. I helped her out and then we ate together and talked in Italian. Vee Toner was there and she asked me if Vee was my mother. I just roared and poor Vee didn't know what I was laughing at. Then I told her and she thought it was pretty funny. She, Elena Zennaro [a competitor in the 200 breaststroke for Italy], was from Venice, but was born in the Cortina and was thrilled when I told her my grandmother was born there. She had on a pin of a gondola and gondolier and I said I thought it was pretty. So, she took it off and gave it to me. Then I gave her an American pin which she loved. She ordered Minestrone. It looked awful when she got it and she only ate part. She was so cute. She threw her hands up and said, "Povera me" (Poor me). Then she told me how terrible the food was here—the Italian food, anyway. So, now I have another souvenir.

Cheerio.

Love,

Me

p.s. The Irish boys live across the street and they're having a helluva water fight. It's really funny. You should hear the lads talk.

How are lane assignments done, and why does it matter?

When swimming officials assign lanes to swimmers, they put the fastest qualifiers in the middle lanes and the slower swimmers in the outside lanes. This gives an advantage to the fastest swimmers, not because the middle lanes are "faster" but because they can see their nearest competitors, while swimmers in the outside lanes can only see the swimmers next to them. Swimming is likely the only sport that does this.

The top seed is assigned to Lane #4.
Second seed to Lane #5
Third seed to Lane #3

Now the top three seeds are in the middle of the pool, and they can see each other.

It is key to be racing next to your prime competitor rather than them swimming two or three lanes away. The swimmer cannot see much beyond the lanes on either side of them and in 1956 there are no swim goggles, which help underwater sighting.

Rounding out the assignments, using the same logic.

Fourth seed to Lane #6
Fifth seed to Lane #2
Sixth seed to Lane #7
Seventh seed to Lane #1
Eighth seed to Lane #8

Lane Assignments for the Final
And who can see whom from their lane

Lane #1	Lane #2	Lane #3	Lane #4	Lane #5	Lane #6	Lane #7	Lane #8
Joan Rosazza	Virginia Grant	Faith Leech	Dawn Fraser	Lorraine Crapp	Marrion Row	Shelley Mann	Natalie Myburgh
USA	Canada	Australia	Australia	Australia	New Zealand	USA	South Africa

"On the Blocks"
100-meter freestyle final

The Women's 100-meter freestyle race
1-December-1956 -8:35 pm.

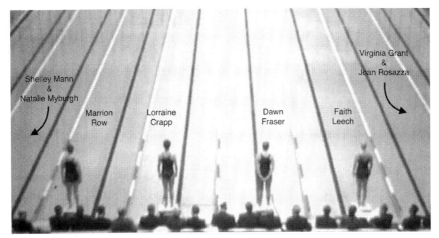

Virginia Grant
&
Joan Rosazza

Shelley Mann
&
Natalie Myburgh

Marrion
Row

Lorraine
Crapp

Dawn
Fraser

Faith
Leech

The Middle Four Lanes

The Final

It has taken two races over the past two days for these eight finalists to make it to the final. Can they do it one more time? Swim their fastest ever? The 5,500 spectators in attendance will know in 66 seconds. Cables and telexes will light up with the results eagerly awaited by family and countrymen, arriving in hours, or in some places not until the next day. The night telegram operator at *The Torrington Register* newspaper in Connecticut has strict instructions to place a telephone call to the Rosazza residence on Riverside Avenue when the cable arrives with the Melbourne results, no matter the time of day or night.

The 100-meter freestyle final was a race within a race. The two Australian superstars, Lorraine Crapp and Dawn Fraser, were the favorites because they were two seconds faster than anyone else in the semi-finals. That is an eternity in a 100-meter race.

Crapp and Fraser may as well have been swimming a two-person race. They had each set a world record leading up to the games, and Crapp was the current record holder. Unless they floundered, the rest of the field was swimming for bronze.

Two swimmers wore bathing caps, Joan Rosazza and Marrion Row. Short hair styles were de rigueur. Of course, no one wore goggles.

On the signal, "Take Your Mark," Virginia Grant and Dawn Fraser were the last to jackknife down. Then, when everyone else was still, Fraser slowly raised her arms behind her in an airplane pose. This wasn't a move of intimidation because none of the other swimmers could see it. It was possibly a ritual of relaxation, or one of anticipation. Overall, the three Australians used the airplane pose, while the other five swimmers let their arms fall forward, relaxed and pointed toward their toes.

When the gun fired no one was slow off the blocks. The arms-hanging-down swimmers did a windup start by swinging their arms up and around windmill fashion to gain momentum. The Australians swung their airplane arms down and forward in a half circle to start their dive. Neither technique gave an advantage in this race.

The first 25 meters saw no one out ahead. By the turn at 50 meters, Fraser was ahead by a stroke, closely followed by Crapp and Faith Leech. Rosazza was in 6th place at the turn behind Grant and Row. She was breathing to her right, away from the other swimmers. But on the way back she would be looking right at Grant and Leech.

Unexpectedly, Marrion Row of New Zealand did an open turn, which takes longer. She seemed to mistime her last strokes into the wall. She had to take a half stroke with her left arm. The rule was, the swimmer had to touch the wall with their hand before the turn. All the other swimmers did flip turns.

After the turn and into the first couple of strokes, Fraser and Crapp's lead grew to three-quarters of a body length. Leech was third, followed by Grant, while Rosazza and Row were tied for 5th. The open turn cost Marrion Row dearly. Shelley Mann was 7th, one stroke behind Rosazza.

Lorraine Crapp took the lead from Dawn Fraser in the middle of the last length. At this point, she had a faster turnover than Fraser. But then, in the final 15 meters Fraser surged ahead and finished first, 4-tenths of a second ahead of Crapp, in a world record time of 1:02.0.

Meanwhile a three-person race played out in lanes 1, 2, and 3. Rosazza gained on Grant, and Leech faded. With 5 meters to go it came down to the last stroke. Rosazza and Leech touched together, with Grant behind by just her head.

The timers had Faith Leech in third place, 1-tenth of a second ahead of Joan Rosazza, 1:05.1 to 1:05.2. The judges conferred, and after five minutes declared Leech the third place finisher. Rosazza made 4th with a very strong second 50 meters where she caught and passed Grant and Row.

The Australian sweep was met by enormous cheering from the home country crowd and was splashed across the newspapers the next day. The Aussies loved their swimmers and this was their day.

What did this portend for the 4 x 100-meter relay in three days? Were the Australians invincible?

Coming into the finish, Timers and Judges at the ready.

Letter: The Final of the 100-meter freestyle

Monday December 3, 1956

Dear All,

    Thanks for the cablegrams. As you have heard, I was 4th and just missed being 3rd. Several people thought I was 3rd, but that's not the way the judges saw it. Before the meet, I wasn't very nervous. In fact, I had a good time for myself. Our final was after the men's diving final so I didn't swim until 8:30. Shelley [Mann] and I got there about 6:30 because they only let you warm up until 7:00. Then, after warming up, I went into the locker room, changed into a dry suit and put my sweat suit and wool socks on. They have about 14 beds in the locker room so I rested on one of those. Then Natalie Myburgh from South Africa came over and we started talking. Ginny Grant came in and we were talking and laughing. Dawn Fraser breezed in at 7:45 and joined our group. She's very nice. When you have people like that to talk to, it makes things much easier and time really flies. We had all seen the movie "High Society" and we were quoting silly lines from it and we were just roaring.

Shelley [Mann] kept very much to herself. If she would only let herself go, she wouldn't be so nervous. Lorraine Crapp kept to the side too.

At 20 after 8:00, an official came in and told us to line up, so we did. The locker room is at the far end of the pool so we have to parade to the starting blocks. Everyone was pretty tense. The starter got us in a group and told us how it would work. He said, "Now, girls, this is a final." It sounded so silly that I said, "It is?" As though I hadn't known it. He said, "You mean you didn't know?" We all laughed and everyone eased up a bit.

Then we all had to sit on our starting blocks. I was in Lane #1 next to Ginny Grant who was in Lane #2. They had made a mistake on my qualifying time. It was 1:05.9, not 1:05.5 as they had previously announced. So, I qualified 7th, not 5th. When I was sitting on the block as they were announcing us, I said a prayer that I swim so that no matter how I did, I could feel afterward that I had done my very best possible. And that's the way I feel. I'm a bit disappointed that I didn't get a medal, but I guess I didn't deserve one. I did beat Shelley though and if the World Tour comes thru, I may have a chance to join that.

After the race it took them five minutes to decide whether I was 3rd or 4th. Then they had the victory ceremony with the three Australians and three Australian flags. I wanted to send you a cablegram, but the facilities here aren't good. I'd have had to go to the cable office which is 10 miles away. I figured you'd have heard the news by then.

Bill Yorzyk won the men's 200 butterfly and Jack Nelson was 4th. Then Bob Clotworthy won the 3-meter diving, Don Harper was 2nd, and Glen Whitten was 4th (all USA team members).

I got dressed and came up and sat with Stan [Tinkham]. He said he was very pleased with what I'd done and he was proud of me. He said seeing as it was Saturday night, he'd like to take me out—he and Vee [Toner] that is. Shelley [Mann] was supposed to have a date but he never showed up so we asked her to come with us. We took a taxi to the Savoy Hotel which is supposed to be Melbourne's best. Everyone was in evening dress and we had blouses, skirts, and flats on. We got in for the floor show. They had a Philippine band which was great. I ordered spaghetti as did everyone else. Then Stan told the waiter to bring a quart of beer and three glasses. Vee had scotch. Shelley had never had anything to drink before and we made her have a glass of beer. She got very silly and we just had a ball. She didn't have any more to drink. I guess she figured, that was enough for the first time.

Stan and I consumed three quarts of beer between us in a period of four hours. I danced with him too. At 11:30 we went to the first floor where they had another band. We met Mr. Mosler who owns some sort of safe company and I guess he's loaded. He came here just to see the games. He had invited Stan to be his guest and bring some friends. He had the Philippine basketball team there. We talked, ate, and danced. I looked at my watch and it was 1:30 am. Then the party broke up. Can those Philippine boys dance. I learned the Cha-Cha.

All the way home we were silly. Stan told one about the drunk who fell down the elevator shaft and said, "I said up not down!" Then the one about the drunk who was putting his key into the post of the street light and saying, "I know there's someone home There's a light on upstairs." And the drunk who told the policeman, "Of course I'm driving, officer. I can't walk." Pretty good, eh.

Sunday, I went to 9:00 am Mass and then we practiced for half an hour. All afternoon, Murph, Marsh [Mary Ann Marchino], and I played cards with [Hawaiian swimmers] Bill Woolsey, Ford Konno, and George Onekea. It was a lot of fun.

The Duke [of Edinburgh] visited the village and he stopped near our house. We gave him a wave and all yelled "Hi Duke." He waved back. All the Australian women were swooning over him. You'd think he was Elvis or something. He's quite Royal looking.

This morning we practiced from 11:30—12:00. The Hungarians were practicing too. I was talking with Eva Szekely who is the one who speaks English very well. She got second in the 200 breaststroke. Her husband, Dezso, is captain of the Hungarian Water Polo team, but he doesn't dare go back. He is going to America and she said she may never see her husband again. She is going back [to Hungary] to her 4-year-old daughter. Then she winked and whispered that she was going to try and take her daughter out and meet her husband in the US. She gave me a Hungarian Olympic badge which is beautiful. I noticed that part of it was cut off. She said that they cut the star out of their badge. It's the Russian star. That's their revolutionary badge. What a souvenir.

I'm at the meet now. Pat McCormick [USA], came in

1st in the 3 meter diving, Jeanne Stunyo [USA] was 2nd, Irene MacDonald [Canada] was 3rd, and Barb Gilders [USA] was 4th.

The backstroke heats are going on now. Carin [Cone] won her heat—but Mary Ann [Marchino] was 4th in hers. I don't know if she'll qualify for the final.

Cheerio for now.

Love, Me

p.s.   On the way home I plan on arriving in LA at 5:30 am December 12th. I have a reservation for a flight that night at 9:30 pm. This means I'll arrive in NY at 9:00 am. Then I'll go to LaGuardia and take a plane to Hartford. I should get in at about 11:00 or 12:00 noon December 13th. I'll call from NY and let you know when I'm due to arrive.

I'll inform you of any change in planes. We're not stopping anywhere on the way home except to refuel. That will mean 30 hours flying plus a day's wait in LA plus about 12 hours more.

Cheerio.

Love again

Me

Associated Press Telegram to
The Torrington Register after the race

"Melbourne, December 2, Associated Press

Joan Rosazza said today she's now looking forward to the women's 400-meter relay for a chance to win a medal in the Olympics.

Joan was naturally disappointed but not broken up over her fourth-place finish in the women's 100-meter freestyle Saturday night.

'When I came out of the water one of the officials told me he thought I had finished third. So it was a bit of a letdown when the announcement came that I was fourth,' Joan told the Associated Press in the Americans' dining room at the Olympic Village.

'Even so, I felt that I had done my best. My 1 minute, 5.2 seconds time was the best I've ever done, and for the first time I was the best of the American girls in the race,' Joan said.

Joan said that she believed she and Sylvia Ruuska were sure of places on the relay team and that Shelley Mann and Nancy Simons probably would be picked for the other places.

Joan wanted to be sure that her family knew how she came out. When assured that results had been sent to the United States promptly, she said she would give up on the idea of telephoning home, adding that she had been getting plenty of news from her family."

BA008 SPH371 SSN256   1956 DEC 3

B WYA052 (B NP194) LONG NPR COLLECT=AP NEW YORK DEC 2 345P=

REGISTER=

TORRINGTON CONN RTE DIRECT AM=

MELBOURNE, DEC 2-(AP)-- JOAN ROSAZZA SAID TODAY SHE'S NOW
LOOKING FORWARD TO THE WOMEN'S 400-YARD RELAY FOR A CHANCE
TO WIN A MEDAL IN THE OLYMPICS.

¶   JOAN WAS NATURALLY DISAPPOINTED BUT NOT BROKEN UP OVER
HER FOURTH-PLACE FINISH IN THE WOMEN'S 100-YARD FREE STYLE
SATURDAY NIGHT.

¶   "WHEN I CAME OUT OF THE WATER ONE OF THE OFFICIALS TOLD
ME HE THOUGHT I HAD FINISHED THIRD. SO IT WAS A BIT OF A
LETDOWN WHEN THE ANNOUNCEMENT CAME THAT I WAS FOURTH",
JOAN TOLD THE ASSOCIATED PRESS IN THE AMERICANS' DINING
ROOM AT THE OLYMPIC VILLAGE.

¶   "EVEN SO, I FELT THAT I HAD DONE MY BEST. MY 1 MINUTE,
5.2 SECONDS TIME WAS THE BEST I'VE EVERY DONE. AND FOR THE
FIRST TIME I WAS THE BEST OF THE AMERICAN GIRLS IN THE RACE,"
JOAN SAID.

¶   JOAN SAID THAT SHE BELIEVED SHE AND SYLVIA RUSSKA WERE
SURE OF PLACES ON THE RELAY TEAM AND THAT SHELLEY MANN
AND NANCY SIMONS PROBABLY WOULD BE PICKED FOR OTHER PLACES.

¶   JOAN WANTED TO BE SURE THAT HER FAMILY KNEW HOW SHE
CAME OUT. WHEN ASSURED THAT RESULTS HAD BEEN SENT TO THE
UNITED STATES PROMPTLY, SHE SAID SHE WOULD GIVE UP THE IDEA

OF TELEPHONING HOME, ADDING THAT SHE HAD BEEN GETTING
PLENTY OF NEWS FROM HER FAMILY=

ASSOCIATED PRESS NY=

Telegram of Joan's interview after the 100-meter freestyle final

Chapter 10

Birth of the Butterfly

Writers of swimming history disagree on who invented the butterfly stroke. But one thing is certain. Butterfly was not a recognized event at the Helsinki Olympic Games in 1952. It wasn't until the Melbourne Games in 1956 that the butterfly came into being as a new and separate event.

However, experimentation was going on. In the London Games in 1948 all the breaststrokers swam traditional breast-stroke. Four years later in Helsinki all the medal winners in breaststroke swam the butterfly arm stroke combined with the breaststroke "frog" kick, and they were not disqualified. This faster technique was not against the breaststroke rules!

<u>Experimentation in secret 1949-1952</u>

Inside the cloistered world of elite swimming behind the Iron Curtain, Hungarian swimmers were experimenting with the breaststroke. One swimmer in particular, Eva Szekely*,

_____

*   For more on Eva Szekely, see Appendix A, Biographies

was an expert at it. Instead of keeping her arms underwater throughout the breaststroke pull and recovery to the front again, she recovered her arms over the water, a technique she believed was perfectly legal and, was much faster.

Eva Szekely (1927-2020)

BR: *Joan, you met Eva Szekely in Melbourne?*

Joan: *Yes, Eva won the breaststroke in Helsinki in 1952 by doing a butterfly motion with the frog kick and by the book it was legal.*

And Melbourne was the first Olympics with the butterfly as an official stroke.

BR: *So, over the water arm recovery?*

Joan: *Yeah, it was the birth of the butterfly.*

Then, somebody came up with the "dolphin kick." That's what we called it. I think it was someone in the US because we took first, second, and third (in Melbourne) and there were still other swimmers doing the frog kick.

BR: *Yes, Shelley Mann was 1st, Nancy Ramey came in 2nd, and Mary Sears took 3rd.*

Joan: *And not everybody was using the dolphin kick and I mean; they just blew them away. Both kicks were legal as long as your legs were doing the same thing.*

BR: *So, the frog kick was slower.*

Joan: *Exactly, with the overarm, Eva won the gold in 1952 doing the butterfly in the breaststroke event.*

Helsinki, Finland—Swimming competition: 25-July to 2-August, 1952

The hardy Finns decided to build an outdoor swimming pool for the 1952 Summer Olympic Games. Perhaps an outdoor pool with cool temperatures would favor a Scandinavian to win a medal. The weather in August in Helsinki averages 70 for a high and 52 for a low. (21C—11C). The heated outdoor pool was kept at 75 degrees (24C). That's cold for a competition pool. And for a swimmer sitting on the deck, the water feels warm once you dive in—little consolation. Maybe there were Finnish Sauna's in the Olympic Village?

Eva Szekely entered the 200-meter breaststroke. She won the Gold Medal, setting an Olympic Record. She improved her time by nine seconds over her London performance in 1948, (where she came in fourth) swimming traditional breaststroke. Eva Novak-Gerard (Hungary) was second, Elenor Gordon (Great Britain) was third and another Hungarian, Klara Killermann was fourth. The nearest American swimmers were

Gail Peters, 24th, Della Sehorn, 26th, and Julia Cornell, 28th.
No American made it into the semi-finals

200-meter breaststroke Women's Results—1952

Rank	Name	Country	Time
1	Eva Szekely	Hungary	2:51.7 Olympic Record
2	Eva Novak-Gerard	Hungary	2:54.4
3	Elenor Gordon	Great Britain	2:57.6
4	Klara Killermann	Hungary	2:57.6
5	Jytte Hansen	Denmark	2:57.8
6	Mariya Havrysh	Soviet Union	2:58.9
7	Ulla-Britt Eklund	Sweden	3:01.8
8	Nel Garritsen	Netherlands	3:02.1

200-meter breaststroke Men's Results—1952

Rank	Name	Country	Time
1	John Davies	Australia	2:34.4 Olympic Record
2	Bowen Stassforth	United States	2:34.7
3	Herbert Klein	Germany	2:35.9
4	Nobuyasu Hirayama	Japan	2:37.4
5	Takayoshi Kajikawa	Japan	2:38.6
6	Jiro Nagasawa	Japan	2:39.1
7	Maurice Lusien	France	2:39.8
8	Ludovit Komadel	Czechoslovakia	2:40.1

Four years later—Melbourne, Australia

In 1956, the International Olympic Committee added
butterfly as the fourth approved stroke. They tightened up

the breaststroke rules, disallowing the butterfly variant. The 100-meter butterfly was included as an official event for the first time at the Melbourne Games. The breaststrokers reverted back to the traditional form. Now there were four Official strokes: Backstroke, breaststroke, butterfly, and freestyle.

This changed the Individual Medley (IM) event by adding butterfly to round out the discipline to four strokes: butterfly, backstroke, breaststroke, and freestyle. That's the event we see today. Records in the IM were wiped clean and begun again. Before that, the Individual Medley swimmers swam three strokes, backstroke first, starting in the water, followed by breaststroke, then freestyle.

Oddly, there were only 12 women entered in the 100-yard butterfly, apparently because the butterfly was so new. All one had to do was beat four competitors and one made the final!

In the years between 1952 and 1956 butterflyers experimented with the dolphin kick. They swam much faster. The American practitioners, who arrived in Melbourne in 1956 doing the dolphin kick, promptly swept the medals. Shelley Mann took Gold, Nancy Ramey the Silver, and Mary Jane Sears the Bronze. The USA moved from 24th in the breaststroke to 1st in the butterfly in four years. It was a huge turnaround for USA Swimming and a glorious day for Mann, Ramey, and Sears.

Bill Yorzyk of the USA won the Gold Medal in the 200-meter butterfly by a whopping 4.5 seconds (2:19.3), setting an Olympic and World record. The American women and men were now the dominant force in the new butterfly stroke.

Eva Szekely stuck with the breaststroke in Melbourne rather than switch to the butterfly. Eva took the Silver Medal in the 200-meter breaststroke in Melbourne with a time of 2:54.8. Her Olympic Record (2:51.7) set in Helsinki in 1952 was erased from the record books because she had used the butterfly arm stroke, though she he kept her Gold Medal. The Olympic Committee upgraded Hungary's Eva Novak's Silver Medal time of 2:54.0 from Helsinki 1952 as the official Olympic Record because she swam traditional breaststroke. That was the Olympic Record at the start of the Games in Melbourne.

On the Men's side, the breaststroke Olympic Record set in Helsinki by Australian John Davies (2:34.4) was also erased from the record books. Like Eva, he also kept his Gold Medal. What is strange is that the International Olympic Committee did not restore American Joe Verdeur's breaststroke record of 2:39.3 from the London Games in 1948, where he swam traditional breaststroke. Why they overlooked that is a mystery. They went all the way back 12 years to the Berlin Olympic Games and restored Tetsuo Hamuro of Japan's time of 2:42.5 as the Olympic Record at the start of the Melbourne Games.

Chapter 11

World Politics is an Olympic Participant

Eva Szekely, the great Hungarian swimmer, gave her Olympic Patch to Joan Rosazza. The Hungarian athletes' symbolic protest in Melbourne was to cut out the Russian Star from their Olympic patches, as Joan wrote home in her previous letter. A similar snipping-out took place back home where the Hungarian Flag was flown with a hole in the middle where the Russian Star used to be.

The revolt at home began as a student demonstration on October 23, 1956, then it spread throughout Hungarian society for two-and-a-half weeks, ending with a brutal Russian crackdown on November 10th. The Hungarian Uprising spilled over at the Melbourne Olympic Games shortly after Hungarian Olympic Team arrived in Melbourne in November 1956. In the Olympic Village the Hungarian athletes took down the Hungarian Flag and raised the Free Hungary flag in its place.

They came with little else than the clothes on their backs. When the Hungarian team arrived in the Olympic village and met their fellow athletes, they were welcomed and made to feel at home. These Games were known worldwide as the "Friendly Olympics."

Russian Star cut out
in protest by
Hungarian athletes

The Hungarian Olympic Patch, given to Joan Rosazza by Eva Szekely

However, the men's Water Polo match between Hungary and Russia was marred by fighting between the two teams. One Hungarian player was struck in the eye by a Russian player. He was taken out of the match to stem the bleeding, thus the headline, "Blood in the Water Match" appeared in newspapers around the world.

The whole match was bedlam from the start. The rough play escalated throughout, and then, with one-minute remaining, and with Hungary ahead 4-0, the match was stopped and the win was awarded to them. This was not only because of the altercations between the players, but for reactions from angry spectators.

Hungary went onto win the Gold Medal in the final against Yugoslavia, 2-1. It was to become the most famous water polo match of all time.

There were reasons aplenty to boycott these Olympic Games, none of which involved Australia. Here's a list of the three boycotts:

- The Netherlands, Spain, and Switzerland boycotted the Games because of the Soviet invasion of Hungary.
- The People's Republic of China boycotted because Taiwan was allowed to compete.
- Egypt, Iraq, and Lebanon boycotted in response to the Suez Canal Crisis.

*Hungarian Flag with the Russian
Coat of Arms cut out*

Chapter 12

Challenging the Undefeated

Letter: Waiting for the Relay

Tuesday December 4, 1956

We practiced lightly for the relay. Then we watched the swimming and diving in the afternoon and evening. Our relay qualified 3rd. Betty, Kay, Nancy [1:05.5], and Marley [1:05.6] swam. Because Nancy beat Marley, she'll swim the final.

That night we had a rip-roaring water fight in our apartment. P.J. and Jeanne had water pistols and they were squirting Barb, Syl, and me. Juno was out. So, we got cups full of water and threw them at them. They all locked me out of the apartment. I was determined to get back in. So, I walked away from the door and sneaked back so they couldn't see me. I barged in the door and got about three cups full of water right in the kisser. By the time the fight ended, there was about a foot of water on the bathroom floor.

-Joan

Wednesday December 5, 1956

We practiced lightly. I met Eva Szekely at the pool. She told me how she had stayed up all night waiting for word from Hungary about her 4-year-old daughter. Relatives of hers were trying to get her daughter out. Then Eva and her daughter would go with her husband to America. They didn't get the child out so now Eva has to return. That's really risky. Betty Brey is going to sponsor a 28-year-old Hungarian girl who is going to the States.

Nancy Ramey met Suzie Ordogh[*], a 16-year-old Hungarian swimmer who received word that both her parents were killed. So, Susie can't go back. Nancy wrote her parents and told them about Suzie and they wrote back and said that they'd like to take Suzie into their home. That's really something.

-Joan

Qualifying for the Relay Final

For this event there was a qualifying swim and then a final swim two days later. Ten teams, representing ten countries, were entered.

Australia qualified in first place. Only the top eight teams moved onto the final.

1. Australia	4:25.0	*Swam two alternates in heats, resting Dawn Fraser and Lorraine Crapp*
2. South Africa	4:26.8	*Same four swimmers in heats and the final*

---

[*]   For more on Suzie Ordogh, see Appendix A, Biographies

3. USA	4:27.3	*Swam three alternates in heats, giving all six swimmers a chance to swim*
4. Germany	4:27.5	*Same four swimmers in heats and the final*
5. Hungary	4:28.1	*Same four swimmers in heats and the final*
6. Canada	4:29.3	*Not known*
7. Sweden	4:30.1	*Not known*
8. Great Britain	4:34.6	*Not known*
9. Japan	4:35.8	*Did not make the final*
10. France	4:36.6	*Did not make the final*

The American Team Members in the Final

Sylvia Ruuska—At 15 years old and 5' 10", Sylvia was the youngest member of the relay. She was the American Record Holder in the 400-meter freestyle and winner of the US Trials in that event. She was a distance freestyler, but possessed a sprinter's speed. Later at the Games, Sylvia won the Bronze Medal in the 400 freestyle, coming in behind the two Australian super stars, Lorraine Crapp and Dawn Fraser.

Shelley Mann—An all-around swimmer who came in 6th in the 100 free five days earlier. Later in the Games, Shelly won the Gold Medal in the 100-meter butterfly in an Olympic Record time of 1:11.0 as part of a USA sweep of the event.

Nancy Simons—The winner of the 100 freestyle at the US Trials. Nancy was the only USA swimmer to swim both the qualifying heat and the final of the relay. (More on how the coaches picked the swimmers for the Qualifying and the Final is below.)

Joan Rosazza—Swam in the anchor position against Lorraine Crapp, silver medalist in the 100-meter freestyle five days earlier.

Joan Rosazza at Yale University

The Australian Strategy:

The Australian coaches chose this order for their swimmers in the final: Dawn Fraser, Faith Leech, Sandra Morgan, and Lorraine Crapp.

One could say that Australia's strategy of leading off with the fear-inducing Dawn Fraser was tactically smart—get a big lead, then, hold on until the anchor leg, where Lorraine Crapp could bring home the race. It was simple. With a lead, and clear open water ahead, the 2nd and 3rd Aussie swimmers could maintain it. Of course, if any other relay team could stay close to Dawn Fraser, the plan might backfire. Like the starter's gun did when it fired a second time right after the start of the race.

The American Strategy:

The American coaches chose this order for their swimmers in the final: Sylvia Ruuska, Shelley Mann, Nancy Simons, and Joan Rosazza.

The Americans had six swimmers officially qualify for the relay at the US Olympic Trials. The first, second and third place swimmers in the 100 freestyle from the trials, plus three more swimmers chosen by the coaches. It was tradition to give all six swimmers a chance to swim at the Olympic Games. The American coaches thought that they could easily qualify for the finals with three alternates swimming in the qualifying heat. And they accomplished that. The USA team qualified 3rd and they would swim next to the Australians in the final, a crucial first step.

Gold and silver medals were up for grabs and it was an edge-of-your-seat, experience for the standing room only crowd.

The Final

A medal for the USA was not guaranteed. And neither were the Australians guaranteed a gold medal. Only 3.1 seconds separated teams one through five. It was unclear how the final would play out because of the use of alternates in the qualifying heats by the Aussies and the Americans. One day passed between qualifying and the final. It was crucial for USA to swim next to the Aussies, where they could see them.

Lane Assignments for the Final

Lane #1	Lane #2	Lane #3	Lane #4	Lane #5	Lane #6	Lane #7	Lane #8
Sweden	Hungary	USA	Australia	South Africa	Germany	Canada	Great Britain

The next day's Melbourne newspaper, *The Age* published the following article covering the relay final.[*]

Melbourne, December 7, 1956 by reporter Bruce Welch:

World Record in Women's Relay
By Bruce Welch

"The girls provided the thrills...in the relay. "Past the post" was the popular opinion before the race but they had to fight all the way to beat off a surprisingly strong United States challenge.

The Gold Medal was in doubt in the third leg when

---

[*]   Copyright © 1956, *The Age* newspaper, Melbourne, December 7, 1956 by reporter Bruce Welch, used with permission

14-year-old Sandra Morgan lost some ground in her first lap. But she fought back grandly to hand over to Lorraine Crapp a half-yard clear. And that was that.

Lorraine was tagged by American Joan Rosazza in the first 50-meters but drew away on the return to win by two yards. Dawn Fraser led off for Australia with a 1:04.2 "leg," which was two seconds slower than her best and did not give us the lead expected. The reason, Dawn explained later, was the accidental firing of a second cartridge by the Starter—Mr. George King. "I saw the girls beside me head off, and when I heard the second shot, I popped up to see if the rope had been lowered for a false start." Dawn said. "I got going again but it did set me back." Official explanation of the incident was that the Starter was cleaning the gun and accidentally discharged it. The error certainly set Australia back as America's first swimmer, Sylvia Ruuska normally would not have got so close to Dawn.

Faith Leech started brightly in the second stage but weakened on the return as game little Shelley Mann fought hard for the USA. Faith's time on my watch was 1:05.3 also below her best but she still had a two-yard advantage at the change. Nervous young Sandra Morgan went very hard but Nancy Simons swam brilliantly for the Americans to turn very slightly ahead. Momentarily, it looked as though Lorraine Crapp would be forced to give away a lead on the last "leg." However, Sandra swam with amazing spirit to force herself up to her rival with 15 yards to go and forge a half-yard ahead at the end. She clocked a 1:04.9 on my watch, her best swim to really clinch the Gold Medal—for there was no one left to match Lorraine in the last lap.

Joan Rosazza, who told her teammates days ago

they could swim a world record and win, tried hard and stuck with Lorraine for 50-meters but she just lacked the brilliance. "We tried to talk ourselves into winning and we very nearly did," said Joan. "We figured we'd have to break a world record—we broke the old one—but it just wasn't good enough. We figured if we did our best time ever, we might win it, but the Australians were just too good."

And no wonder, Lorraine whisked through in 1:02.7, just 0.7 seconds outside of the world 100-meter world record of Dawn Fraser to win by two yards.

The final time of 4:17.1 broke the world record set by an Australian team last month. The only change last night was the substitution of Sandra Morgan for Margaret Gibson. The previous time was 4:28.7. The American girls, whose aggregate best time before the event was a 4:23.0, swam a 4:19.2 in second place to also break the month-old world mark."

~~~~~~

Final Results

Gold	Australia	4:17.1 *(World and Olympic Record)*
Silver	USA	4:19.2 *(USA National Record)*
Bronze	South Africa	4:25.7

Letter: The 4 x 100 freestyle relay

Thursday December 6, 1956

We rested all day for the relay.

The Frankie Laine show with drummer Buddy Rich, Stan Freberg (comedian), and Eileen Barton (singer) was in Melbourne and they put the show on at the village. It was free. The cast ate in our dining hall.

We swam the relay. Before it, we were in the locker room and all the teams were talking and singing. We had a couple of uke's too. Dawn Fraser is a riot. The English girls sang some really funny songs, ("Oh, Sir Jasper"). The South Africans and Canadians were fun too. With everyone joking, it was easy on the nerves. The relay itself was very exciting. With the Australians taking the first three places in the 100 free, they expected to win by over half a length [25 meters]. Sylvia had to swim Dawn Fraser who only did 1:03—Syl did 1:06.5. Then Shelley swam Sandy Morgan... Australia's slowest. Shelley really caught up a lot. Then Simons swam Faith Leech and she caught up almost even with her. Lorraine Crapp swam last with me. You should have heard the crowd. They were screaming at the top of their lungs. Lorraine and I were about even at the turn. I was just giving it everything I had. I stayed with her until the last 15 meters when I couldn't give it any more.

They said that it was the best race of the games. I was very disappointed I hadn't been able to beat Lorraine, but everyone really made me feel good. I couldn't walk for 10 minutes after the race my legs were so weak. We got our beautiful medals while they played "God Save the Queen."

The Prince of Denmark [Prince Axel] presented the medals. After that, we came back to the village and ate at the International Dining Room. The bus ride back was funny. There were a whole bunch of Russians on it. We started singing, "Here's to ____[fill in name]____ and the way he does the Hula Hop" to all the Americans and each one had to do a Hula. Then we started singing it to the Russians and they got up and did what they thought we were doing. It was just a riot.

At the dining hall, we ate with the Russians. Only about three could speak English and these were coaches or managers. The athletes could speak only Russian. Everyone had Spaghetti and milk. There is a Russian diver, Brenner, who is married and has a 9-year-old son. He had a crush on Jeanne Stunyo and he told the interpreter that he wanted Jeanne to come to Moscow. Then Juno said, "What's he planning on doing with his wife?" A boy (24 years) from the American team said, "They can send her to Siberia." The Russian said, "I beg your pardon—what did you say?" The guy didn't answer and everyone just sat there. It was very quiet. I thought it was pretty funny. Then everyone started talking again with no further mention of the incident.

After dinner, a whole bunch of us got together. It was in the greatest apartment. We had all the divers except Pat. Sylvia and I were the only swimmers. Jeanne is just a riot. She's a devil too. She sneaked into the British dining hall and stole a quart of the Duke's table wine. She was 2nd on the low board diving and Barbara Gilders was 4th. Juno was 2nd on tower and P.J. 3rd. No one in our apartment got worse than 4th. Anyway, that night we got the Duke's wine and 10 of us split it. We only got about a thimble full apiece but it was fun. Then we started walking around the women's compound and someone called us over. It was the British girls. Their chaperone made them be in bed even though they had finished competing. They had some cokes and they invited us in. They were on the first floor so we climbed through the windows. Otherwise, we would have had to pass the chaperone's door.

We were talking and laughing. All of a sudden, we heard these footsteps come clomping down the hall. We were so silly. We held the door—at least three of the other kids did. I was laughing too hard. Finally, everyone was laughing so hard she got in. She stood in the middle of the floor saying, "Get out, get out, get out of here." Still laughing, we scrambled out the windows and ran around the side of the building. We all mimicked her "Get out." The next day we saw the British kids and they told us that after we left, she stood there and gave them a lecture and while she was talking, they could hear us imitate her. They said they were biting the blankets to keep from laughing.

One of the girls on the Great Britain team is from Scotland. Her name is Frances Hogben. I gave her one of my tank suits and she's going to send me an emblem from Scotland. After the competition I got to meet and know people a lot better. During competition everyone kept to herself and had to train certain hours—etc. Everyone wants the American tank suit. I gave another to a Hungarian. I gave both my caps away—one to a French girl. It's so nice to give things to those people because they really appreciate it. Back to Frances, she swam the 100 free and didn't make the final. I love to hear her talk. She rolls her r's. It's fascinating.

After the episode we wandered around some more

and then went to bed at 2:00 am. June Irwin [10 meter platform diver] insisted on going with us, even though her final was the next day. She had qualified 6th in the preliminary and came in 2nd in the final, so she did very well.

-Joan

Postscript on the relay

When a swimmer is asked, "What goes through your mind in a swim race," they say, "nothing," or "a million things." They can hardly hear anything because of the white noise from the water. They can barely see across one or two lanes to the left and right.

But, if they do see someone ahead of them, they can chase them, like children do when there is no official race, and there are no medals.

"How did a girl raised in a town with no sports for girls get to stand on the medal box at the Olympic Games and receive a Silver Medal from the Prince of Denmark? Not on her own."

- Joan Rosazza

Everything, all the emotion, all the effort, was left in the pool that day. Then came Prince Axel of Denmark with the medals. These girls would be home for Christmas.

USA Relay Medalists pose with their medals.
L-R: Joan Rosazza, Nancy Simons, Shelley Mann, Sylvia Ruuska

Joan's Silver Medal

Chapter 13

Olympic Village Life

Letter: "Up on the roof"

Friday December 7, 1956

The last day of competition. In the afternoon they
had the water polo finals between Russia and Hungary.
The Hungarians hate the Russians with a passion. It's
vice versa, I guess. The Hungarians were ahead 4-0 and
a brawl started. A Russian hit a Hungarian above the
eye and opened a huge cut. They finally broke it up and
played a bit more. It started again and they called the
game off and gave the win to Hungary. The crowd was
very pro Hungary.

That night, Shelley won the butterfly, Nancy was
2nd, and Mary Jane was 3rd. George Been lost the 1500
and Pat won the tower dive, Juno 2nd, and P.J. 3rd. After the meet, most of the kids went to the Savoy Hotel
as guests of Mr. Mosler who had given us the party after
the 100. I was a bit tired from the previous night, so I
decided to stay in the village where they were having a
dance. I got back from the pool at 11:00 or so and went

95

to the dance with Gladys Priestly, Sara Barber [Canadians], and Sylvia [Ruuska]. We wore Bermudas. It wasn't much fun so we all decided to go to bed. I stopped in at the apartment downstairs and there were Carin [Cone], Nancy Ramey, and Mary Anne [Marchino] just sitting around writing and talking.

No one was around but us, so we decided to do something to Vee [Toner]. We thought of short sheeting the bed and all the usual tricks but we wanted to do something different. In Vee's room is a wardrobe cabinet, dresser, bed, chair, rug, etc. She keeps all her stuff in the wardrobe cabinet. By stuff I mean chocolate bars which we were supposed to have gotten but Stan [Tinkham] said we couldn't eat chocolate—or gum too. (What a sentence.) We couldn't steal the candy bars because the cabinet was locked. We decided to take the whole cabinet. We took it outside and were trying to decide what to do with it when I spied the roof of this shed which is just in front of the apartment. It was kind of heavy so I ran up to the gate and got one of the guards. By the way, they doubled all the guards because of the feared danger to the Hungarians who had remained behind.

One of the guards came by and he passed up furniture to the three of us on the roof. The bed was a bit heavy so we took it apart and re-assembled it on the roof. There was nothing left in the room and everything was arranged on the roof as it had been in the room. You've never seen anything so comical in your life. Girls from different countries would come by. As soon as they noticed it, they'd burst out laughing. It was about 12:00 am, so I went to bed. I was too tired to wait up for Vee, though I would have given a lot to see her when she first saw it.

The party from the Savoy came in at 5:00 am and they made enough noise so everyone woke up. Vee was so funny. When they first saw it, they didn't know whose furniture it was. Then Vee found out. You'll never guess what she did. She put her sweat suit on, climbed up on the roof and slept there.

The next morning it was the talk of the village. Newspaper reporters were there and people crowded outside the fence to see it. I have a couple of pictures of it.

Joan

The next day the Vee Toner story made the front page of *The Sun-Herald*, Sidney, Australia.

Vee Toner's Recap of the Women's Swimming and Diving Competition

News Bulletin #5
January 18, 1957

We went, we saw, we conquered. The 1956 Olympic Women's Swimming and Diving Team was one of the greatest as our wonderful victory has proven to the world. You said, "Bring home the bacon" and we did. Our eighteen excellent representatives, two fine coaches, and your splendid support are responsible for our victory.

On November 9, 1956, we departed for Australia ready for vigorous competition ahead. However, we had two glorious days in Hawaii which served as a very needed relaxation. We continued our practice sessions at Honolulu on a slightly lighter schedule. We arrived in Melbourne on November 13th and continued with two practice sessions every day with time-out for church on Sunday mornings. With so many nations present (33), and swimmers (235) our swimming practices were limited to one hour per session.

All the girls knew they had a great mission and their hearts were set on the Olympic Victory Stand. If not a medal, they were doing their best to be among the first six in the unofficial point scoring used by all nations. The girls accomplished their objective by finishing with nineteen places in medal and scoring positions, three gold medals, eight silver, and three bronze, plus three fourth places, one fifth, and one sixth.

There was a USA clean sweep of the medals in the platform diving event. The USA team proved to be a very strong one, however, all of you as well as the team members will go along with me in paying special tribute to Pat McCormick, the greatest woman diver the world has ever known. Pat was the Gold Medal winner in both the springboard and platform diving in the Helsinki Games in 1952 and gained the "grand slam" again in 1956 in Melbourne.

It has been a pleasure to serve you and my congratulations to all of you in the USA who have worked so diligently for women's swimming and diving and thus made this great victory possible. I also thank so many of you who sent cards, notes, letters, and cables. I read all of these to the entire group at our evening meeting before the start of the swimming competition. The final letter I read was from the White House, "The best of luck to you and the members of the Olympic Women's

Swimming and Diving Team.," and it was signed by President Dwight D. Eisenhower.

-Vee Toner, Manager and Chaperone, USA Women's Swimming and Diving Team

Vee Toner—USA Women's Olympic Swim Team Manager and Chaperone

Letter: A merry old time

Saturday December 8, 1956

Everyone slept all morning because of the late-night hours. Murph, Marsh, and I went to 8:00 am Mass. We had to go then because December 8th isn't a Holy Day in Australia, so there were no late Masses.

That afternoon was the closing ceremony but no Americans went. We all figured it would be a bit anti-climactic. Instead, we went to take Sauna baths. We brought the Finnish woman who takes care of the Sauna some perfume. Jeanne Stunyo had her camera and we got some great pictures. They're really funny. The Sauna was hot—210 degrees.

Saturday evening was a swim meet at the Olympic pool. It was a FINA meet and you represented your continent. In the locker room before the meet, I was with four Japanese girls. They're very sweet looking. I don't speak Japanese and they spoke only a little English but it was fun trying to understand each other. I've learned to talk a lot by motions. I'd try to say or ask something and they'd look puzzled. Then all of a sudden, they'd understand and their faces would light up and they'd shake their heads and laugh and we'd all laugh. One of them took out of her duffle bag a little box. It had a glass lid which she removed. The box itself is beautiful. Although it's just plain wood, it's all fitted and there's not a nail in it. There's a small barrel in the box and inside are two Japanese dolls. It's quite a treasure.

I swam 50-meter freestyle and was 3rd. Boy did I feel rotten. With all these adventures and late hours, I did a 29.8 which wasn't tooooo bad.

Immediately before the race I was talking to a Mexican swimmer. I had sort of met her before. I had seen her around the village. The night after the 100 free trials a bunch of us were coming home on the bus. She was sitting all alone in the front seat and her head was down. The bunch of us had a uke and we were singing away. Charlie Roeser, one of the men's managers, said that the Mexican girl was probably homesick, so we all walked to the front of the bus and serenaded her. We finally got a smile.

While we were talking Saturday night, she told me that she hadn't done a good time in the 100-meters and everyone at home would be disappointed in her. Mexico sent three girls to the games—two swimmers and one fencer and they expected each to do her best time. The girl's name is Blanca Barron. She said she knew her parents weren't disappointed but everyone else would be. She said the newspapers would be down on her. I know what she means because people are that way. They expect so much and then act disappointed when their expectations don't come thru. This is especially true in the field of sports. It takes a lot to please a so-called sports fan.

After the meet we went to a party at one of the Australian diver's house. It was fair—very crowded. We got there at 12:00 and left at about 2:00. Shelley [Mann], Nancy [Simons], Lenore Fisher [Canadian], and Blanca Barron [Mexico] came home in a cab. We had a merry time singing and giving the cab driver a rough time.

-Joan

Letter: Yachting

Sunday December 9, 1956

Got up at about 8:30. We were invited by the Victorian Ladies Yachting Club to go to the beach. We had a ball. It was too cold to swim, but we made the best of the situation. Murph, Marsh, and I went to 11:00 Mass. One of the club members took us. Then we got back and Murph and I went for a row boat ride and nearly tipped the boat. We ate lunch and afterwards went for a 3-hour ride on a 44-foot yacht. That's the life. We just lay on the deck in the sun. They have surf in Melbourne like Hawaii, only really not as nice. I steered the yacht for a while—big deal.

That night was a party at John Marshall's [former Yale swimmer]. All the American swimmers and divers were there and that's all. John's wife is great. They have a 5-month-old son. I left early—12:00 am because I was still tired from parties, etc.

-Joan

Monday December 10, 1956

The boy swimmers left for home, so the parties kind of ended. Early in the morning a bus came and took anyone who wanted to go to the animal sanctuary. They have animals out in the open and you can pet them, etc. We saw emus and kangaroos, and I had someone take movies of me with a koala. I was furious when I found the film was stuck in the camera. They would have been great movies.

That evening was a trophy meet. Our apartment kids were the only ones on the ball. We were the only ones to enter the meet. When we got there, we were glad to have entered. They had beautiful prizes. I entered the 100 butterfly, My first length was beautiful. I beat everyone—even Shelley [Mann]. However, I died on the second lap and came in last—there were four in the race. They had a relay and put all the kids from different teams together. We only had to swim 50-meters apiece. Believe it or not, our relay won and I got a beautiful alarm clock. Everyone in Apartment #3 won something beautiful. The others were green with envy.

-Joan

Letter: The Frankie Lane Show

Tuesday December 11, 1956

The big day to pack and leave. I rushed around like crazy to get packed and did some last-minute shopping. I got home at 4:00 after rushing around. Murph came running up to me said that our plane had been delayed in Hawaii and they had to fly a new motor from the mainland. Instead of leaving at 7:00 pm, the 11th, we would depart at 4:00 pm the 12th. What a disappointment when you've been planning on leaving. Everyone was joking around saying we should have been stuck in Hawaii on the way home.

However, everyone made the most of the situation. The boys—Stan, Glen, Dave [canoers], Dick [field hockey player] played volleyball against Pat, Juno, Jeanne,

Barb, and me. We couldn't mix the boys with the girls because we used the fence of the girl's compound for a volley ball net. We used a soccer ball for the volley ball. It was a bit heavy. The boys played men's rules and we played girls rules. We played two games—and the boys won the first and we won the second.

That night we hopped into cars and got into the Frankie Lane show for free. They gave us front row seats and cracked jokes about us all thru the show. It was closing night and they really messed around. Great show! We talked with the cast after dinner. I got Buddy Rich's autograph for Tom. He's a great drummer. Then we went back to the village and played "Sardine" which is similar to Hide and Seek.

Then to bed, Joan

Chapter 14

Going Home

Letter: Melbourne—Fiji—Hawaii

Wednesday December 12, 1956

I changed my LA—NY flight. Nothing too exciting. We completed last minute packing and hopped buses. The plane left at 4:00 on schedule. My seat mate was Mary Jane Sears. She slept most of the way and was kind of air sick.

-Joan

Thursday December 13, 1956

Stopped in Fiji for an hour and a half. It's really warm.

-Joan

Wednesday December 12, 1956—International Date Line

We stopped in Hawaii at 4:00 pm. They said our plane would be delayed until 8:00. We were going to go to the beach, but decided there wouldn't be time. After dinner the word came that we'd leave at 9:00 am because there was something wrong with the engine.

We stayed at the Waikikian, a brand-new hotel with tons of atmosphere. We walked along the beach to the Royal Hawaiian—then came back and went in the ocean at 10:00 pm. Then we had dinner and slept like a log.

-Joan

Letter: Long Flights Home for Christmas

Thursday December 13, 1956

We got up and ate breakfast. At breakfast they told us the plane wouldn't leave until 11:00 and we'd leave the hotel at 10:00. Oh! I had the most delicious banana pancakes for breakfast. We put suits on and swam and sun bathed until five of ten. We got to the airport at 10:30 and they announced we wouldn't leave until 1:00. It was getting to the point where no one cared what happened. I had made arrangements to fly from LA and because they changed the time again, I was in trouble.

Here's the biggest joke. Wednesday night when we got in the Mexicans were just leaving for LA I talked to Blanca Barron for about 15 minutes. This morning I got to breakfast and there was Blanca. The Mexicans had flown five hours out of Hawaii and had to come all the way back. That's 10 hours of flying and they got nowhere. They were 15 minutes from the point of no return. The pilot and crew didn't want to alarm the passengers so they didn't tell them they were returning. Just about the time they should have been landing in LA they heard the announcement that they were arriving in Honolulu Hawaii in 20 minutes.

We finally took off at 2:00. It's now 10:45 pm Los Angeles time and we are due to arrive in LA at 12:50 am. We just heard that the international airport in LA is closed because of bad smog. This means we'll have to land at Burbank airport and stay overnight in LA There are no planes out of LA so everyone has to stay.

Cheerio

-Joan

Homecoming

A throng of residents greets Joan outside Torrington City Hall after she was presented the Key to the City by Mayor William T. Carroll. A military band played, and civic groups did what they do best.

A month later a testimonial dinner was held at the Torrington YMCA. It was an appropriate venue. Joan received a set of golf clubs: a one, three, and five wood, from the organizers of the affair. A gift of a new car had been under consideration, but the limit for gifts to amateur athletes in 1956 was $50. Any gift over that amount would disqualify them from participating in future amateur sport events, including the Olympic Games.*

---

* After the Paris Summer Olympic Games in 1924, Doris Murphy, Joan's first swim coach, worked as a camp counselor at Fort Ticonderoga, Lake George, New York. Her amateur status came into question and was reviewed afterwards, but in the end, her status was left intact.

Joan arrives at the train station in New Haven, Connecticut on December 14, 1956 and is greeted by her parents, Agatha and Aldo Rosazza.

Joan receiving the Key to the City of Torrington

Aldo, Joan, and Agatha Rosazza at Torrington
City Hall December 16, 1956

Homecoming Float, December 16, 1956.

Chapter 15

Sixty Years On

60th anniversary of the 1956 Team
USA Olympic Trials 2016

Carin Cone Vanderbush, (USA backstroker at the 1956 Melbourne Games) organized the gathering. Carin also planned the outfits. Bright blue jackets, white slacks and white shoes.

It was held at the 2016 USA Olympic Swimming Trials in Omaha Nebraska. Ten Olympians from that team were honored one evening. Joan is third from the right waving as she is introduced.

Later, Joan removed the buttons from her jacket and gave one button each to the Purdue University women swimmers who were participating at the trials that weekend.

Ten members of the 1956 USA swimming and diving team
who were feted at the 2016 Olympic trials

Purdue University Women's Swim Team, and a Varsity Jacket is awarded

In the photo on the following page, Joan is in the middle with the Purdue Women's swim team members who were swimming in Omaha, and their coach, John Klinge. Joan is sporting her new Purdue varsity swim jacket, given to her by the team all these 60 years later.

There were no varsity letters for women swimmers at Purdue in 1956 because the women's swim team wasn't recognized. Now it had come full circle.

Joan in the middle with Purdue University women swimmers on either side.
Purdue University Women's Swimming team coach John Klinge on far right.
Taken in Omaha at the 2016 Olympic trials

Chapter 16

Joan and her Brothers

Bishop Peter Rosazza and Jack Rosazza

BR: *Let's talk about the airmail letters that Joan wrote home from Australia. Joan wrote a letter the day before the big race, a letter on the day of the race, and another letter the day after the race. Those letters were trickling back to Torrington over the Pacific. But you already knew the results. So, how did that feel when you read the letters?*

Jack: *Well, we knew that Joan wasn't very happy there... Having a hard time adapting... (sarcasm) (laughter)*

Joan: *(laughs) Homesick.*

Peter: *I was in the Seminary in Rochester, New York.*

Jack: *And I was home in Torrington.*

One thing is the time of year that the Olympics were—November, December. That was a really strange thing. But most of what I remember are things like Joan's picture in the New York Times.

There was joy in the letters. I wrote down seven words that stuck out to me: "Youth, Enthusiasm, Energy, Humor, Appreciation,

Wonder, and Joy." They show up so strongly.

Joan: *Thank you. I'm humbled. (laughs) ...It was one adventure after another.*

Peter: *Joan was quite a star when she came home. She even made Jeanne Colbert's radio program.*

Joan: *Every morning on WTIC (Hartford), and you were with me.*

Peter: *That was a big show though. A lot of people listened to that show.*

Joan: *And she'd go, "Huh-Huh-Huh" (imitates Jeanne's laugh, the pitch of her voice rising on every syllable)*

Peter: *(imitating) "Huh-Huh-Huh" (laughter)*

I was in Rochester in seminary. One day somebody came and knocked on my door. It was a seminarian and he said, "What did you tell the Rector?" So, I went down to his office and he said, "Look! Look!"

He was so pleased. He had seen the picture of Joan in the New York Times.

Then, I think it was in 1957, Joan was in Purdue and she took the train home, and it stopped in Rochester NY. She got off the train and took a cab to the seminary and a couple of the seminarians said, "Your sister's here! Your sister's here!"

We went to Mass and Joan was in the back of the church. Of course, all the seminarians walking past were looking over, "Who is this?"

After Mass Joan said, "I haven't had anything to eat since yesterday at eight o'clock."

So, comes the Rector, and I said, "I'd like you to meet my sister Joan."

"Oh, Miss Rosazza, I'm sooooooo pleased to meet you," he replied.

Then I said, "She hasn't eaten."

"Come right with me," he said.

The two of us were following the Rector. He walked into the priests' dining room. That was the FIRST time a female went into the priests' dining room. I'll never forget that. Joan broke tradition.

BR: *Were you surprised that your sister won an Olympic medal?*

Peter: *Joan, you said you would rather run track.*

Joan: *Yes.*

Peter: *But you had the opportunity with the swim team and Doris Murphy. You practiced in this little tub in Torrington. I'd read newspapers and magazines at the time and would see swimmers like Shelley Mann, and others who came from these swim clubs, who did have training, and good coaches. The very fact that you went to Detroit for the Olympic trials and you made the team, that was sensational, coming from where you did.*

Joan: *I never thought of it, Peter.*

I wanted to say one thing. Our parents raised us to be independent. I think they really did. We had a lot of freedom. We were encouraged to go our way.

Peter: *We stuck together as a family. We helped each other out. I think that shows the greatness of this family.*

Jack: *Our parents were not hovering parents. They did not spend any time watching us at swim practice. They were not devoting their entire life to us. They really let us go, let us do our thing.*

I didn't expect Mom and Dad to be at every swim meet, every game that I had. And it didn't hurt. You didn't go home and say, "Why weren't these people there?" Today it is so different.

Joan: *I remember mom saying, "Well now you have something to talk about at supper." (laughter)*

BR: *You mom was a teacher in Torrington?*

Joan: *Yes. In the mid-1950s, after Tom, our baby brother, was well settled in school, Mom wanted to go back to teaching. When she applied for a teaching position, she was told she would be allowed* *to substitute teach in Torrington, but not teach full-time because she was a married woman.*

God forbid!

I'm not sure if that was a Torrington rule only.

They started a Special Education program that was held in a room at the YMCA. In November that year, they came to her and asked if she was interested in teaching it. Three people between September and November had resigned. She took the job, and went on to get a Master's Degree in Special-Ed. In the mornings, she had 24 children for four hours, 20 minutes for lunch, then ten more for two and a half hours, and there were no aides back in those days.

BR: *You mom and dad came to Detroit for the trials?*

Joan: *Our grandfather had just died and Mom and Dad hadn't planned to come, but, at the last minute, they did.*

Jack: *Our family never went on vacation. We didn't have the money.*

We never went to the Nationals in Florida to see Joan. The only time I left the state (of Connecticut) was when I was on the high school swim team. We went to New Englands. Our 1955-56 swim team was so good that we swam against college freshmen teams, Dartmouth, UConn, Navy, and Yale, with more wins than losses.

BR: *Jack and Peter, can you talk about your swimming backgrounds.*

Jack: *I was swimming at the Y one day, and Ray Ostrander was there. He was a natural, once in a lifetime swimmer. Renni Belli, (the coach) said to Ray, "You can come on the swim team," then he looked at me and said, "Oh, you can come too." (laughter)*

My best event was the Individual Medley—all four strokes. We were doing butterfly in 1958-1959.

Peter: *Swimming was big for me, but there was no high school team. I remember some of us talking to the School Superintendent and the Athletic Director about starting one. The year after I graduated, (1952) there was one. I went to Dartmouth and was on the* *freshman team. My specialty was backstroke and the Individual Medley (IM). But there was no butterfly. You started the IM with backstroke, in the water, and only three strokes were used, (backstroke, breaststroke, and freestyle).*

Joan was an all-around athlete. She was an excellent golfer. She had prowess, intelligence...and guts.

Joan: *You never...none of you, ever said I couldn't do this sport because I was a girl. And I think a lot of women heard that. It was not something you do. I had all of you standing by me all the way.*

One evening after supper I ran outside to play with the neighborhood gang and there were two young women almost my age, sitting on the back steps next door with their grandmother. She saw me running out to play and she said, "Shame on you." I'll never forget that. It was like a dagger.

Jack: *If you were raised in Iowa, where I live, there was organized basketball for girls. The Iowa State Basketball Championships for girls has been held ever since the 1920s. They played six on six basketball. The games were attended by thousands and thousands of moms and dads, brothers and sisters.*

Joan: *If I lived in Iowa, I would have been a basketball player.*

Jack: *You would have been great, Joan.*

Joan: *Well... (laughs)*

BR: *Jack, can you talk about the Big 10 swim meet between Purdue and Iowa in 2016 when Joan visited?*

Jack: *Did the Purdue coach contact you about going to the meet, Joan?*

Joan: *No, I contacted him. I saw the swim meet coming up and I said this is a twofer. I can see my brother and the Purdue swimmers.*

Jack: *It wasn't just Joan that got to sit on the Purdue bench with the women swimmers, I did too. The swimmers were a thrill to watch.*

Everybody came up to just touch Joan. It was beautiful. All just to have a piece of Joan.

Joan: *Watching the meet, event after event, they were ready to go so soon. Right after they touched the finish the next group went off—boom. We used to slouch up to the blocks. (laughs)*

Peter: *And Joan, you finally got your Purdue letter.*

Joan: *Yes.*

Chapter 17

Reflecting Back, Looking Forward

Joan: *The Olympics at that time were the only total international competition. One had to be an amateur athlete, couldn't take money for competing, and couldn't get gifts worth over $50. Professional athletes weren't paid very much, there was no satellite TV, no TV in many countries, and many had a second job after their season. College greats in basketball, Bill Russell and KC Jones, had just graduated from San Francisco University, signed with the Boston Celtics, and after the Games flew to Boston, having missed part of the season. The Olympic Committee eventually changed that rule and professionals could compete. However, there are many international games now, plenty of places to compete. Not all athletes want to be Olympians. Nancy, Dougie, and I used to sit at the dining table in the Olympic Village with the non-swimmers. Also, at the table besides Bill and KC, was Willye White, I believe she was only 16, who had placed in her track event, the long jump. She eventually became tops in her events for many years. After someone at the table mentioned Willye placing, Bill looked up from eating and with a dry face said, "I'm not impressed," which broke everyone up laughing.*

Gone is the part that I loved, being in the same place with almost all the athletes. Nowadays, many elites have a condo somewhere else, fly in only for their event, or just don't go.

Pappy had a sign in our Purdue locker room. "You have to have the desire." For 4 years, my goal had been to make the Olympic team. That was the desire that drove me. It was part of every practice, and every nationals that I swam in. In the spring of 1957, after the Olympic Games, I was competing in a swim meet at AAU Nationals in Dallas. During qualifying in the 100-yard freestyle, I missed touching the wall with my hand, I paused to touch, then continued. Because of that, I didn't make the final. Then, I realized, I didn't care. I had lost that edge, that desire that had driven me before. In my days as a competitive swimmer at Purdue there were no dual meets, just nationals, and I believe, a state meet for swimmers of any age. I was ready to move on with my life.

Now, we've raised two children. They are in their twenties. We are so blessed. Motherhood, hardest thing I have ever done and the best thing I've ever done.

Chapter 18

Epilogue

The 1956 Olympic Games were the last to be held with no next-day TV coverage around the world. Telegrams were the most immediate mode of communication. At the Rome games in 1960, film from the day's events were flown to New York overnight. Commentary was added to the film in New York and the events were broadcast on TVs across the United States that evening.

Satellite TV was first successfully tested in July of 1962. In 1964, for the first time, the Opening Ceremony of the Tokyo Olympic Games was broadcast live, via satellite, to the United States. The Olympic Games became an instantaneous live event, never to return to the sleepy pre-Telstar Satellite days.

In many ways, Melbourne was similar to other Olympic Games. For example, there was a protest filed at the Springboard Diving competition when the Hungarian and Russian judges secretly agreed to pause too long before flipping over their scorecards, after certain diver's dives. Influence and collusion were alleged, but not proven. There were boycotts: over the Russian invasion of Hungary, over Taiwanese athletes being allowed to compete, and over the Suez Canal crisis. There were defections; 37 Hungarian athletes received political asylum in the United States after the games.

Melbourne was from another era. Drug testing for anabolic steroids wasn't introduced until Montreal in 1976. Professional athletes were not allowed until the 1980s. Swimming events were timed with stop watches and there were no touchpads in the pool.

The participation by women at the Olympic Games greatly increased, as seen in this chart.

	Melbourne 1956	Rio de Janeiro 2016	Rio de Janeiro Paralympic Games 2016
Nations sending athletes	72	207	159
Male athletes	2,938	6,179	2,657
Female athletes	376	5,059	1,671
Total athletes	3,314	11,238	4,328

The amateur athletes came from all across the world to Melbourne; from small towns, big cities, YMCA's, Sports Clubs, high schools, colleges and universities, state sponsored sports systems, and US Army swimming pools. What they had in common was a desire to excel and a dedicated coach.

Dick Papenguth, when he wasn't producing national champion swimmers, taught children with disabilities to swim.

Doris O'Mara Murphy, gave children swimming lessons in the ocean in summer, in New London, Connecticut. After she passed away, her ashes were scattered from a small boat offshore where she gave swim lessons, while a cassette tape of the theme song from "Chariots of Fire", by Vangelis, was played.

Swimming is a sensory deprivation sport. You can bare-ly hear, can hardly see, and must knowingly breathe. Some find it boring because you can't talk to anybody. If you dive too deep, your ears might hurt. A wave can knock you over.

But, from Marco Polo to water polo, Water is Life.

Biographies

The Coaches and Manager:

Doris O'Mara Murphy went to her second Olympic Games in Amsterdam in 1928, but this time as a member of the coaching staff. Later in life Doris taught children how to swim at Ocean Beach Park in New London, Connecticut. She also officiated at local AAU swim meets. In retirement she joined a women's synchronized swim team in Southern California, one of her great joys. Doris died in 1997 at the age of 88.

Dick Papenguth continued to coach men's and women's swimming and diving teams at Purdue University, and produced water carnivals until his untimely death from a car accident at age 67. Dick advocated for people with disabilities and taught many to swim at Purdue and, in the summer, at the Lafayette Country Club. Three of his women's teams won the national AAU championships before women's swimming was an official NCAA sport. He was inducted into the International Swimming Hall of Fame posthumously in 1986.

Stan Tinkham coached just two more years at the Water Reed therapeutic swimming pool, because the growing Army hospital patient population required more access to the warm healing waters. He was instrumental in building a new pool at the Northern Virginia Athletic Club, and in founding the Montgomery County Swim League for age group swimmers. He retired from coaching in 1988 after 33 years. Stan died in 2019 at the age of 87.

Vee Toner's list of accomplishments is long. She was the first woman to umpire tennis matches at US Nationals, and the first American woman to be a chair umpire at Wimbledon. Vee was a lifetime member of Delta Zeta Sorority, and their 1969 Woman of the Year. She was known internationally as a swimming champion and official. Also, she was a distinguished alumnus of the University of Pittsburgh, and inductee to the Pennsylvania Sports Hall of Fame. As the beloved manager of the Olympic team in 1956 Vee became the calming and organizing influencer to these talented, young women. Vee died in 1995 at the age of 88.

~~~~~~

The Swimmers:

Sylvia Ruuska made the USA Olympic Team in 1960 and swam in the preliminary heat of the gold medal winning 4 x 100-meter freestyle relay. Sylvia held the world record in two events in the late 1950s, the 200-meter and 400-meter Individual Medley.

Shelley Mann turned to swimming at age 10 after contracting polio and suffering paralysis in her left leg. She became one of the best all-around swimmers of the 1950s. She won the gold medal in the 100-meter butterfly at the Melbourne Games. She held 10 world records in swimming and was inducted into the International Swimming Hall of Fame in 1966. Shelley died in 2005 at the age of 67.

Nancy Simons Peterson attended Northwestern University in Evanston, Illinois a year before the Olympic Games, to take advantage of swim coaching there. After the Olympics, she transferred to Stanford University, where she received several degrees, married, and worked for many years in research while also raising two children. After retiring she grew interested in genealogy and eventually became a certified genealogist.

The second edition of her genealogy book, Raking the Ashes, Genealogical Strategies for Pre-1906 San Francisco Research (2009) is still used today.

Dawn Fraser became one of only three swimmers in history to win the same event at the Olympic Games three times: the 100-meter freestyle in Melbourne, Rome in 1960, and Tokyo in 1964. She broke the world record for the 100-meter freestyle ten times and she held the record for 15 years until it was broken in 1972.

Eva Szekely, the great Hungarian swimmer and holocaust survivor, along with her Olympic team member and husband, were not able to flee Hungary immediately after the Olympic Games, as so many of her countrymen did. While they competed in Melbourne, their four year old daughter, Andrea, was back home in Hungary. Eva later became a pharmacist and swimming coach in Budapest. Her daughter, Andrea Gyarmati, became a decorated Olympic swimmer, and both mother and daughter were later inducted into the International Swimming Hall of Fame. Eva died in Budapest in 2020 at the age of 92.

When **Suzie Ordogh Zimsen** was at the Olympic Games in Melbourne it was reported to her that her parents were killed in Hungary during the revolution. It turned out that this was false. Her parents survived and they lived to see Suzie become a US citizen, get married, and raise five children. Immediately after the Olympics Suzie went to the USA and was sponsored by American swimmer Nancy Ramey's parents in Washington state. Suzie earned a degree in Chemical Engineering and had a career at The Boeing Company. She is retired and lives with her husband in the Pacific Northwest.

After the Olympics, **Joan Rosazza** finished her studies at Purdue, started teaching in Evanston, Illinois, and eventually moved back to her roots in New England.

Joan continued teaching high school Physical Education and Health in Massachusetts. She also coached girls soccer, gymnastics, and field hockey. Joan was a strong advocate for girls sports throughout her career.

She and her wife have raised two children. Joan is retired from her teaching career, and they live on Cape Cod in Massachusetts.

The Olympic Pin Quiz

A tradition at all Olympic Games is athletes swapping pins with other athletes.

What follows is Joan's collection of Olympic Pins, 25 in all. See if you can guess the nation's names. Hint: There could be more than one pin per nation. Answers in Appendix G.

First, here is the USA Olympic Pin for 1956.

A

blue cross on white field

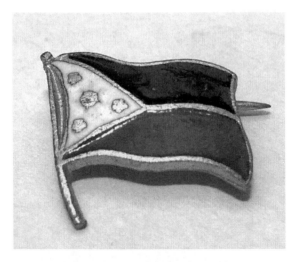

B

*gold stars and sun on white chevron
bicolor of blue on top, red on bottom*

C

white flame and gold torch

D

red star on blue shield

E

tricolor, top to bottom: green, yellow, red

F

gold emblem on blue background

G

arching stripes of green, white, red

H

white sunburst on blue canton, red field

I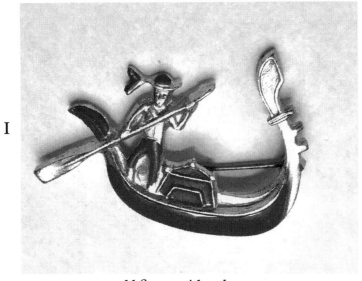

gold figure with red accents

J

gold links with red background
area of blue background below

K

*green tree with 3 flags in sequence: a blue cross on red field
followed by a blue cross on white field, ending with a yellow
cross on blue field*

L

red background with gold laurel

M

red field with gold accents

N

gold crest with red background

O

gold wolf on blue background

P

gold kangaroo

Q

multicolored leaf

R

red star, blue background, red flame and white tent

S

stripes of white, green, and red behind gold crest

T

blue letters on teal background bordered by white gear

U

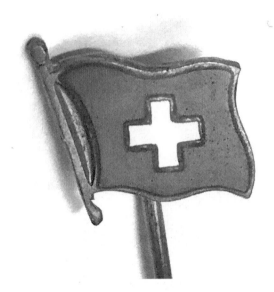

white cross on red field

V

gold elements on green background

W

gold emblem

X

green filled lettering below a red disc on white field

Y

red flame above green country outline
set within a red border with gold text

Appendix C

Sweeping the Podium

Australian women, (Dawn Fraser, Lorraine Crapp, and Faith Leech) swept the first three places in the 100-meter freestyle at the Olympic Games. How often does this occur in Olympic swimming? Since 1920 it has occurred 28 times across 167 events in 13 Olympic Games.

In the 1980s, responding to clamor, the Federation Internationale de Natation (FENA), the international ruling body for swimming, created a new rule for the 1984 Olympic Games in Los Angeles: No country can enter more than two swimmers per individual event, by gender to the Summer Olympic Games.

Inexplicably, this same constraint was put in at the Rome Olympic Games in 1960, but just for those Games and none thereafter until 1984.

The intent is to prevent medal sweeps by one country, giving other countries a chance for a medal. Did this new rule target the United States, or East Germany and the USSR after their eight medal sweeps in the 1980 Games?

Below is a chart of all the sweeps, Gold, Silver, and Bronze, by year between 1920 and 1980. The United States chalked up 23 of 36 sweeps during that period. Of the 13 Olympic Games the US participated in no other country swept more than two events.

Olympic Year	Total # events	Events Swept	USA	Japan	Australia	Soviet Union	East Germany
1920	8	3	3				
1924	9	3	3				
1928	9	1	1				
1932	9	1		1			
1936	9	0					
1940 (canceled)	0						
1944 (canceled)	0						
1948	9	1	1				
1952	9	0					
1956	11	3	1		2		
1960	11	0					
1964	13	3	3				
1968	24	5	5				
1972	24	2	2				
1976	22	6	4			1	1
1980*	22	8				2	6
Total	189	36	23	1	2	3	7

What does this say about the increased pressure at the US Olympic Trials? Only the first and second place swimmers at the trials make the team in any single event except for relay, where the top six finishers qualify. The pressure on the top level swimmers at the trials is immense, possibly more so than at the Olympic Games.

~~~~~~~~~~

*   The USA boycotted the 1980 Olympic Games held in Moscow.

Appendix D

Awards

*Joan's Olympic Games Diploma
for 4th place in the 100-meter freestyle*

In April, 1956 some members of the Lafayette Women's Swim Club traveled to Daytona Beach, Florida for a swim meet. Four women from the team, including Joan Rosazza, set a world record in the 4 x 100-yard freestyle relay. This is the FINA certificate of that event. The swimmers are: Joan Rosazza, Lucy Crocker, Barbara Love, and Helen Hughes.

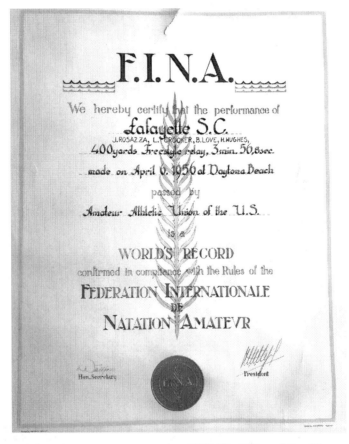

FINA World Record Certificate,
4 x 100—yard freestyle relay, record time of 3:56.8

World record setting relay team—1956 Daytona Beach, Florida
L-R: Joan Rosazza, Lucy Crocker, Barbara Love, Helen Hughes

Doris Murphy's telegram of congratulations to Joan
on her world record swim with her teammates

Appendix E

Memorabilia

USA Women's Olympic Swim Team, Melbourne 1956
Front row, L-R: Dougie Gray, Joan Rosazza, Kay Knapp, Corin Cone, Mary Anne
Marchino, Shelley Mann, Pat McCormick
Standing, L-R: Stan Tinkham, Juno Irwin, Maureen Murphy, Nancy Ramey, Marley
Shriver, Jeanne Stunyo, Nancy Simons, Barbara Gilders, Mary Jane Sears, Betty Brey,
Sylvia Ruusla, Paula Jean Myers, Glenn McCormick, Vee Toner

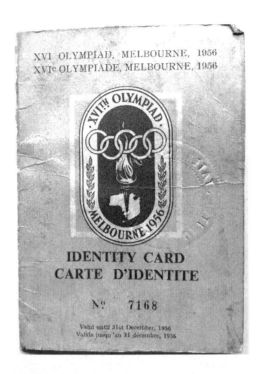

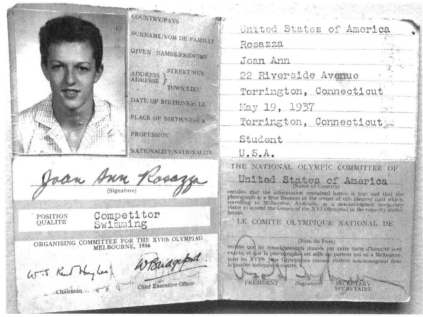

Olympic Village ID Card—Melbourne

Amateur Athletic Union (AAU) National Champion Patch

USA Olympic Uniform Beret

Small Souvenir Boomerang

Olympians member patch

Joan in Lane #7 in the air after the starting gun in an undated photo

"Y" SENIOR MERMAIDS

Above are shown the members of the Y.M.C.A. senior girls swimming team. They are: front row, left to right, Sandra Ruwet, Alice Fitch and Colleen Murphy. Back row, Joan Roasazza, Susan Mignerey, Maureen Murphy and Anne Caravati. Shirley Minor and Claire Cummings were missing when the photo was taken. (Thurber photo)

Torrington YMCA Senior Girls Swim Team Members
Front L-R: Sandra Ruwet, Alice Fitch, Colleen Murphy
Back L-R: Joan Rosazza, Susan Mignerey, Maureen Murphy, Anne Caravati
(not pictured: Claire Cummings, Shirley Minor)

Torrington Y stand out swimmers
at a Waterbury, Connecticut Swim meet in 1952
L-R: Sandra Ruwet, Eileen Murphy, Joan Rosazza, Claire Cummings

Mexico's 1956 Olympic Games pennant

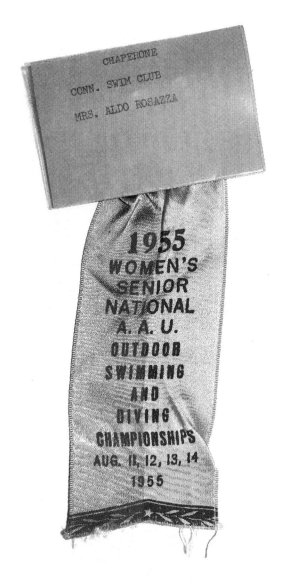

Chaperone badge
Ms. Agatha Rosazza (Joan's Mom) AAU Nationals swim meet 1955

Olympic village meal card

Olympic Souvenir lunch bag

35th Annual
YALE
SWIMMING CARNIVAL

PAYNE WHITNEY GYMNASIUM

Saturday, February 23, 1957 -- 8:15 p.m.

YAA5657-55

Cover of the program for the 35th Annual Yale Swimming Carnival, 1957

Yale University Swimming Carnivals

Bob Kiphuth, Yale Men's Swimming Coach, 1918-1959, created swimming carnivals in 1920. They were fund raising efforts for the swimming program. Other Universities picked up on the trend, including Dick Papenguth of Purdue University.

What follows is a sampling of the program from the Swimming Carnival at Yale held on February 23, 1957.

Highlights described below are: Connecticut high school swimmers competing in a medley relay, Carin Cone Vanderbush attempting to break a USA backstroke record, Joan Rosazza swimming an exhibition race, and a spectator favorite, comedic diving, where two elite divers shock and amaze the crowd with death defying dives.

Selected Events[*]

Event No. 2—Medley Relay—Connecticut High Schools

(A sample of teams from the Naugatuck Valley League)

NAUGATUCK HIGH SCHOOL
Ken Teach, Bill Fulton, Bill Swick.
Alternate—Tom McDermott
Coach: John Carr.

SACRED HEART HIGH SCHOOL
Adolph Birkenberger, William Kelly, Terry Hebert.
Alternate—Pat Bergin.

[*]   Transcribed from the Yale Carnival Program, Joan Rosazza collection.

Coach: Jim Farrar

TORRINGTON HIGH SCHOOL
Don Mills, Don Will, Don Baker.
Alternate—David Ryan
Coach: Charles Duggan

Event No. 4—Cairn Cone—Backstroke Record Attempt

Existing Record—75 yard backstroke: 48.4. Set by Maureen O'Brien of the Newark Athletic Club on March 30, 1949.

Miss Cone was a member of the United Stated Olympic Team at the recent Games in Australia. She placed second to Judy Grinham of Great Britain in the 100-meter backstroke with an identical time of 1:12.9. She has set records in the 200-meter backstroke swimming for world and American recognition, and the 100-meter backstroke for meet and American Records. Miss Cone, who swims unattached, is from Ridgewood, New Jersey.

Event No. 5—Joan Rosazza—Exhibition

A resident of Torrington, Connecticut, Miss Rosazza was a member of the United States Olympic Team in Australia this past year where she placed fourth in the 100-meter freestyle. She holds the Connecticut state freestyle records in the 40, 50, 100, 200, 220, 250, 440, and 500 yards. She was a member of the All-American team in 1955, and set an American record for 100 yards over a 20 yard course. She swam the anchor leg on a world record freestyle relay team at Daytona Beach in 1956.

Event No. 8—Diving Exhibition—Patricia Keller McCormick

Mrs. McCormick, Sullivan Award winner and nation's number one athlete for 1956, scored double Gold Medal victories in both the 1956 Olympic Games in Melbourne, Australia, and the 1952 Games in Helsinki, Finland. She has been diving competitively since 1946, and holds twenty-seven national championships, as well as her international honors. She is equally at home in competition off the one-meter, three-meter, or in platform diving. Coached by her airline navigator husband, Mrs. McCormick is the mother of a ten-month old son, and makes her home in Lakewood, California. She attended Long Beach College, and is affiliated with the Los Angeles AC.

Event No. 13—Comedy Diving—Bruce Harlan and Hobie Billingsley

Two of the nation's top divers with a repertoire of the funniest comedy board-to-water antics in the business. Both were standouts while undergraduates at Ohio State, incubator of a long list of collegiate diving champions. Harlan won more major diving titles than anyone else in the world, twenty in the United States, and more in international competition in England, Holland, Belgium, Ireland, France, Bermuda, and North Africa. He won the Olympic Springboard Championship in London in 1948. He is presently diving coach at the University of Michigan. Billingsley was an all-star athlete competing in tumbling, trampoline, and diving at Ohio State. He won the Western Conference and National Collegiate diving championships and was a member of the All-American diving team for four consecutive years. He won international honors in Bermuda over a three-year span, and is rated one of the nation's outstanding comedy divers.

Appendix F

References

Chapter 2: Joan's First Coach

O'Mara Murphy, interview by George A. Hodak, *An Olympian's oral history : Doris O'Mara Murphy, 1924 & 1928 Olympic Games, swimming,* LA84 Foundation, 1988. https://digital.la84.org/digital/collection/p17103coll11/id/227/

Chapter 5: The Earthquake in Women's Sports

Miller, Bryce, "Christine Grant joins Register's Iowa Sports Hall of Fame," *Des Moines Register* (Des Moines, IA), Oct. 9, 2013.
https://www.desmoinesregister.com/story/sports/columnists/bryce-miller/2013/10/09/christine-grant-iowa-sports-hall-of-fame/2955685/

Draisey, Brooklyn, "UI legend reflects on 50 years of fighting for gender equality in intercollegiate athletics," *The Daily Iowan* (Iowa City, IA), Oct. 9, 2018. https://dailyiowan.com/2018/10/09/ui-legend-christine-grant-title-ix-gender-equality-field-hockey-grant-field/

Chapter 10: Birth of the Butterfly

Official Report of the 1952 Olympic Games, LA84 Foundation, 1955
https://digital.la84.org/digital/collection/p17103coll8/id/4192

Appendix G

Photo Credits

Chapter 1, page 4: Courtesy of *The Torrington Register Citizen*, Torrington, Connecticut.

Chapter 2, page 10, top: Courtesy of Eileen Murphy Mooney.

Chapter 2, page 10, bottom: Courtesy of Eileen Murphy Mooney.

Chapter 6, page 24: Courtesy of Joan Rosazza:

Chapter 7, page 29: Courtesy of Joan Rosazza:

Chapter 7, page 30: Courtesy of Joan Rosazza.

Chapter 7, page 36: Courtesy of Joan Rosazza:

Chapter 7, page 40: Courtesy of the Melbourne Olympic Organizing Committee.

Chapter 8, page 49: Courtesy of Joan Rosazza. Photo: Bill Ryan.

Chapter 9, page 60: Courtesy of the Melbourne Olympic Organizing Committee.

Chapter 9, page 61: Courtesy of the Melbourne Olympic Organizing Committee.

Chapter 9, page 64: Courtesy of the Melbourne Olympic Organizing Committee.

Chapter 9, page 70: Courtesy of Joan Rosazza. Photo: Bill Ryan.

Chapter 10, page 72: Photo of Eva Szekely, Anefo (Algemeen Nederlandsch Fotobureau), CC0, via Wikimedia Commons.

Chapter 11, page 78:Courtesy of Joan Rosazza. Photo: Bill Ryan.

Chapter 11, page 79: Photo of Hungarian flag with Russian coat-of-arms cut out, The American Hungarian Federation, Attribution, via Wikimedia Commons.

Chapter 12, page 84: Courtesy of Joan Rosazza.

Chapter 12, page 93: Courtesy of the Melbourne Olympic Organizing Committee.

Chapter 12, page 94: Courtesy of Joan Rosazza. Photo: Bill Ryan.

Chapter 13, page 99: Courtesy of the Delta Zeta Sorority, 202 East Church Street, Oxford, OH 45056

Chapter 14, page 108, top: Courtesy of Joan Rosazza.

Chapter 14, page 108, bottom: Courtesy of Joan Rosazza.

Chapter 14, page 109, top: Courtesy of Joan Rosazza.

Chapter 14, page 109, bottom: Courtesy of Joan Rosazza.

Chapter 15, page 112: Courtesy of Joan Rosazza.

Chapter 15, page 113: Courtesy of Joan Rosazza.

Appendix B, pages 131—144: Courtesy of Joan Rosazza. Photo: Bill Ryan.

Appendix D, page 147: Courtesy of Joan Rosazza. Photo: Bill Ryan.

Appendix D, page 148: Courtesy of Joan Rosazza. Photo: Bill Ryan.

Appendix D, page 149, top: Courtesy of Joan Rosazza.

Appendix D, page 149, bottom: Courtesy of Joan Rosazza. Photo: Bill Ryan.

Appendix E, page 151: Courtesy of Joan Rosazza.

Appendix E, page 152: Courtesy of Joan Rosazza. Photo: Bill Ryan.

Appendix E, page 153, top: Courtesy of Joan Rosazza. Photo: Bill Ryan.

Appendix E, page 153, bottom: Courtesy of Joan Rosazza. Photo: Bill Ryan.

Appendix E, page 154, top: Courtesy of Joan Rosazza. Photo: Bill Ryan.

Appendix E, page 154, bottom: Courtesy of Joan Rosazza. Photo: Bill Ryan.

Appendix E, page 155: Courtesy of Joan Rosazza.

Appendix E, page 156: Courtesy of *The Torrington Register Citizen*, Torrington, Connecticut.

Appendix E, page 157, top: Courtesy of *The Torrington Register Citizen*, Torrington, Connecticut.

Appendix E, page 157, bottom: Courtesy of Joan Rosazza. Photo: Bill Ryan.

Appendix E, page 158: Courtesy of Joan Rosazza. Photo: Bill Ryan.

Appendix E, page 159, top: Courtesy of Joan Rosazza. Photo: Bill Ryan.

Appendix E, page 159, bottom: Courtesy of Joan Rosazza. Photo: Bill Ryan.

Appendix E, page 160: Courtesy of Joan Rosazza. Photo: Bill Ryan.

Appendix H

Answers to the Olympic Pin Quiz

A. Finland
B. Philippines
C. Rominia (Romania)
D. USSR—Russia
E. Ethiopia
F. India
G. Hungary
H. Burma (Myanmar)
I. Italy
J. Czechoslovakia
K. Norway-Finland-Sweden
L. Philippines
M. USSR—Russia
N. Singapore
O. Rome, Italy promotional pin for the 1960 Olympic Games
P. Australia
Q. Canada
R. CCCP—USSR—Russia
S. Bulgaria
T. TP, which means Trudovye Recervy in Russian, and is translated as, Volunteer Sports Society of the USSR
U. Switzerland
V. Pakistan
W. Olympic Games
X. Japan
Y. The Melbourne Olympic Games 1956

Made in the USA
Las Vegas, NV
29 June 2021